INTRODUCTION

Your *Collins Phrase Book* ... ce
guide that will help you ...
clear layout will save yo ... cial
word or phrase.

There are three main sections in this book.

Practical topics arranged thematically with an opening section
KEY TALK containing vital phrases that should stand you in good
stead in most situations.

PHRASES

Short easy phrases that can be adapted for your situation

practical tips are highlighted in yellow boxes

SIGNS ARE IN GREEN BOXES

replies you might hear are highlighted in red boxes

FOOD SECTION

Phrases for ordering drinks and food
A region by region description of French food with a note on
  French wine and other popular drinks
Drinks
Menu reader

DICTIONARY

English-French	French-English	signs highlighted

And finally, a short **GRAMMAR** section explaining how the
language works.

So, just flick through the pages to find the information you need. Why
not start with a look at pronouncing French on page 6. From there
on the going is easy with your *Collins Phrase Book & Dictionary*.

COLLINS

PHRASE BOOK & DICTIONARY

french

HarperCollins*Publishers*

Consultant: Christian Salzedo
Food section by Edite Vieira Phillips

Other languages in the *Collins Phrase Book & Dictionary* series:

GERMAN
GREEK
ITALIAN
JAPANESE
PORTUGUESE
RUSSIAN
SPANISH

These titles are also published in a language pack containing
60-minute cassette and phrase book

First published 1998
Copyright © HarperCollins*Publishers*
Reprint 10 9 8 7 6 5 4 3 2
Printed in Italy by Amadeus SpA

ISBN 0 00-472076 8

CONTENTS

PRONOUNCING FRENCH

We've tried to make the pronunciation under the phrases as clear as possible by breaking the words up with hyphens, but don't pause between syllables.

The consonants are not difficult, and are mostly pronounced as in English: **b**, **d**, **f**, **k**, **l**, **m**, **n**, **p**, **s**, **t**, **v**, **x** and **z**. The letter **h** is always silent, and **r** should be pronounced at the back of the throat in the well-known French way, although an English 'r' will be understood. When **c** comes before the vowels **e** or **i** it is pronounced like 's'; otherwise it is a hard 'k'. Likewise, **g** before **e** or **i** is 'zh' like 's' in 'pleasure', not hard 'g'. The letter **ç** is pronounced the same as **s**; **q** is always like **k** in 'kick' (not the 'kw' sound in 'quick'); **ch** is 'sh'; **gn** is 'ny', something like the sound in 'onion'; and **w** is either 'v' or 'w'. Final consonants, especially **s** and **n**, are often silent, but sometimes not, for example when the following word begins with a vowel – just follow the pronunciation guide.

The sound spelt **ou** in French is something like 'oo' in English, while the sound represented by **u**, which many English speakers have difficulty with, is not really so hard: simply round your lips as if about to say 'ee' but pronounce 'oo'. We use the symbol '<u>oo</u>' in the pronunciation guide. There are two **o** sounds in French; one is something like the 'o' in English 'hope' and one something like 'hop'. We've represented the first by 'oh' and the second by 'o' in the transcriptions. Meanwhile 'uh' represents both the rounded sounds of **peu** and **peur**, and also the sound (like 'a' in English 'ago' or 'sofa') found in **je** and **se** and the first syllables of **retard** and **demain**. Look out for the following letter combinations: **au** and **eau** are 'oh'; **oi** is 'wa'; and **ui** is something like 'wee'.

There are various 'nasalised' vowels in French. When you see a 'ñ' you should nasalise the vowel before it rather than pronouncing an n. For example 'mañ' in the pronunciation guide represents 'm' plus the vowel in the well-known French words **fin** or **rien**, rather than the sounds in English 'man'. The others are 'uñ' (as in **brun**) and 'oñ', which we use to cover the similar vowel sounds in **dans** or **en** or **blanc** and **mon** or **blond**.

*The French are quite formal when addressing each other, especially the older generation. Only use the familiar **tu** form of 'you' to children or to someone you know as a friend. Otherwise it's best to address people as **vous**. Monsieur, Madame and Mademoiselle are used a great deal – use **bonjour Madame** and **bonjour Monsieur** to greet someone, not just **bonjour**.*

yes
oui
wee

no
non
noñ

that's fine
très bien
tray byañ

please
s'il vous plaît
seel voo play

thank you
merci
mehr-see

de rien
duh ryañ
don't mention it

hello
bonjour/salut
boñ-zhoor/sa-loo

goodbye
au revoir
oh ruh-vwar

good evening
bonsoir
boñ swar

excuse me
excusez-moi
eks-koo-zay mwa

sorry!
pardon!
par-doñ

what?
comment?
ko-mañ

*Here is an easy way to ask for something... just add **s'il vous plaît***

a...	**a coffee**	**2 coffees**
un... ('le' words)	un café	deux cafés
uñ...	*uñ ka-fay*	*duh ka-fay*
	a bottle	**2 bottles**
une... ('la' words)	une bouteille	deux bouteilles
oon...	*oon boo-tay*	*duh boo-tay*

a coffee and two beers, please
un café et deux bières, s'il vous plaît
uñ ka-fay ay duh byehr seel voo play

KEY TALK

I'd like...
je voudrais...
zhuh voo-dray...

we'd like...
nous voudrions...
noo voo-dree-oñ...

I'd like an ice cream
je voudrais une glace
zhuh voo-dray oon glass

we'd like to visit Paris
nous voudrions visiter Paris
noo voo-dree-oñ vee-zee-tay pa-ree

do you have...?
est-ce que vous avez...? *[or simply]* vous avez...?
ess kuh vooz av-ay...   *vooz av-ay...*

do you have any milk?
vous avez du lait?
vooz av-ay doo lay

do you have stamps?
est-ce que vous avez des timbres?
ess kuh vooz av-ay day tañbr

do you have a map?
vous avez une carte?
vooz av-ay oon kart

do you have cheese?
est-ce que vous avez du fromage?
ess kuh vooz av-ay doo fro-mazh

how much is it?
c'est combien?
say koñ-byañ

how much is...?
c'est combien...?
say koñ-byañ...

how much is the cheese?
c'est combien le fromage?
say koñ-byañ luh fro-mazh

how much is the ticket?
c'est combien le billet?
say koñ-byañ luh bee-yay

how much is a kilo?
c'est combien le kilo?
say koñ-byañ luh kee-loh

how much is it each?
c'est combien, pièce?
say koñ-byañ pyess

TOMATES.................le KG		TOMATOES PER KILO
POIRES.....................le KG		PEARS PER KILO
ORANGES...............pièce		ORANGES EACH

where is...?
où est...?
oo ay...

where are...?
où sont...?
oo soñ...

where is the station?
où est la gare?
oo ay la gar

where are the toilets?
où sont les toilettes?
oo soñ lay twa-let

DAMES LADIES	**LIBRE** FREE	**ENTRÉE** ENTRANCE
MESSIEURS GENTS	**OCCUPÉ** OCCUPIED	**SORTIE** EXIT

is there/are there...?
est-ce qu'il y a...?
ess keel ee a...

is there a restaurant?
est-ce qu'il y a un restaurant?
ess keel ee a uñ res-toh-roñ

where is there a chemist?
où est-ce qu'il y a une pharmacie?
oo ess keel ee a <u>oo</u>n far-ma-see

are there children?
est-ce qu'il y a des enfants?
ess keel ee a dayz oñ-foñ

is there a swimming pool?
est-ce qu'il y a une piscine?
ess keel ee a <u>oo</u>n pee-seen

there is no...
il n'y a pas de...
eel nee a pa duh...

there is no hot water
il n'y a pas d'eau chaude
eel nee a pa doh shohd

there are no towels
il n'y a pas de serviettes
eel nee a pa de sehr-vyet

I need...
j'ai besoin de...
zhay buhz-wañ duh...

I need a receipt
j'ai besoin d'un reçu
zhay buhz-wañ duñ ruh-<u>soo</u>

I need to phone
j'ai besoin de téléphoner
zhay buhz-wañ duh te-le-foh-nay

KEY TALK

can I...?
est-ce que je peux...?
ess kuh zhuh puh...

can we...?
est-ce que nous pouvons...?
ess kuh noo poo-voñ...

can I pay?
est-ce que je peux payer?
ess kuh zhuh puh pay-ay

can we go in?
est-ce que nous pouvons entrer?
ess kuh noo poo-voñ oñ-tray

where can I...?
où est-ce que je peux...?
oo ess kuh zhuh puh...

where can I buy bread?
où est-ce que je peux acheter du pain?
oo ess kuh zhuh puh ash-tay <u>doo</u> pañ

vous pouvez acheter des billets au kiosque
voo poo-vay ash-tay day bee-yay oh kee-osk
you can buy tickets at the kiosk

when?
quand?
koñ

at what time?
à quelle heure?
a kel uhr

when does the train leave?
quand part le train?
koñ par luh trañ

when does the film end?
à quelle heure finit le film?
a kel uhr fee-nee luh feelm

when does it open?
ça ouvre à quelle heure?
sa oovr a kel uhr

when does it close?
ça ferme à quelle heure?
sa fehrm a kel uhr

yesterday
hier
yehr

today
aujourd'hui
oh-zhoor-dwee

tomorrow
demain
duh-mañ

this morning
ce matin
suh ma-tañ

this afternoon
cet après-midi
set ap-ray mee-dee

tonight
ce soir
suh swar

DU LUNDI AU SAMEDI	WEEKDAYS *(Mon-Sat)*
DIMANCHE ET JOURS FÉRIÉS	SUNDAYS/HOLIDAYS
OUVERT	OPEN
FERMÉ	CLOSED
TOUS LES JOURS	DAILY

LUN.	MON
MAR.	TUE
MER.	WED
JEU.	THU
VEN.	FRI
SAM.	SAT
DIM.	SUN

is it open?
est-ce que c'est ouvert?
ess kuh say oo-vehr

is it closed?
est-ce que c'est fermé?
ess kuh say fehr-may

le musée est fermé le lundi
luh moo-zay ay fehr-may luh luñ-dee
the museum is closed on Mondays

GETTING TO KNOW PEOPLE

*The equivalent to Mr is **Monsieur**, and Mrs or Ms is **Madame**.
The word for Miss is **Mademoiselle**.*

how are you?
comment ça va?
ko-mañ sa va

fine, thanks, and you?
très bien, merci, et vous?
tray byañ mehr-see ay voo

my name is...
je m'appelle...
zhuh ma-pel...

what is your name?
comment vous appelez-vous?
ko-moñ vooz ap-lay voo

I don't understand
je ne comprends pas
zhuh nuh koñ-proñ pa

do you speak English?
est-ce que vous parlez anglais?
ess kuh voo par-lay oñ-glay

MONEY – changing

BANQUE	BANK
DISTRIBUTEUR DE BILLETS	CASH DISPENSER

French banks are open from 9am to 12pm and from 2 to 4pm and closed on either Mondays or Saturdays (as well as Sundays). You can use your bank card and UK pin number to withdraw cash from autotellers with the appropriate logo.

where can I change money?
où est-ce que je peux changer de l'argent?
oo ess kuh zhuh puh shoñ-zhay duh lar-zhoñ

where is the bank?
où est la banque?
oo ay la boñk

where is the bureau de change?
où est le bureau de change?
oo ay luh boo-roh duh shoñzh

when does the bank open?
la banque ouvre à quelle heure?
la boñk oovr a kel uhr

when does the bank close?
la banque ferme à quelle heure?
la boñk fehrm a kel uhr

I want to cash these traveller's cheques
je voudrais changer ces chèques de voyage
zhuh voo-dray shoñ-jay say shek duh vwa-yazh

what is the rate...?
à combien est...?
a koñ-byañ ay...

for pounds
la livre sterling
la leevr stehr-leeng

for dollars
le dollar
luh do-lar

I want to change £50
je voudrais changer cinquante livres
zhuh voo-dray shoñ-zhay sañ-koñt leevr

where is there a cash dispenser?
où est-ce qu'il y a un distributeur de billets?
oo ess keel ee a uñ dees-tree-boo-tuhr duh bee-yay

I'd like small notes
je voudrais des petites coupures
zhuh voo-dray day puh-teet koo-poor

spending – MONEY

In France major credit cards are widely accepted in shops, hotels, restaurants, motorway petrol stations and some hypermarkets. Some French card-reading machines may not be able to cope with the magnetic strip on UK cards, and you may have to show your passport to confirm your identity.

how much is it?
c'est combien?
say koñ-byañ

where do I pay?
où est-ce qu'il faut payer?
oo ess keel foh pay-ay

I want to pay
je voudrais payer
zhuh voo-dray pay-ay

we want to pay separately
nous voulons payer séparément
noo voo-loñ pay-ay se-pa-ray-moñ

can I pay by credit card?
je peux payer avec ma carte de crédit?
zhuh puh pay-ay a-vek ma kart duh kray-dee

do you accept traveller's cheques?
vous acceptez les chèques de voyage?
vooz ak-sep-tay lay shek duh vwa-yazh

how much is it...?	**per person**	**per night**	**per kilo**
c'est combien...?	par personne	par nuit	le kilo
say koñ-byañ...	*par pehr-son*	*par nwee*	*luh kee-loh*

are service and VAT included?
le service et la TVA sont compris?
luh sehr-veess ay la tay-vay-a soñ koñ-pree

I need a receipt
j'ai besoin d'un reçu
zhay buhz-wañ duñ ruh-soo

do you require a deposit?
est-ce qu'il faut verser des arrhes?
ess keel foh vehr-say dayz ahr

I've nothing smaller
je n'ai pas de monnaie
zhuh nay pa duh mon-ay

keep the change
gardez la monnaie
gar-day la mon-ay

AIRPORT

ARRIVÉES	ARRIVALS
DÉPARTS	DEPARTURES
LIVRAISON DES BAGAGES	BAGGAGE RECLAIM
VOL	FLIGHT
RETARD	DELAY

to the airport, please
à l'aéroport, s'il vous plaît
a la-ehr-o-por seel voo play

how do I get into town?
pour aller en ville, s'il vous plaît?
poor al-ay oñ veel seel voo play

which bus goes to the town centre?
quel bus va au centre-ville?
kel boos va oh soñtr-veel

how much is it...?	**to the town centre**	**to the airport**
c'est combien...?	pour aller en ville	pour aller à l'aéroport
say koñ-byañ...	*poor al-ay oñ veel*	*poor al-ay a la-ehr-o-por*

where do I check in for...?
où est l'enregistrement pour...?
oo ay loñ-rezh-ees-truh-moñ poor...

which gate is it for the flight to...?
quelle est la porte d'embarquement pour le vol à destination de...?
kel ay la port doñ-bar-kuh-moñ poor luh vol a des-tee-nass-yoñ duh...

l'embarquement a lieu porte numéro...
loñ-bar-kuh-moñ a lyuh port noo-me-ro...
boarding will take place at gate number...

dernier appel pour les passagers du vol...
dehrn-yay a-pel poor lay pa-sa-zhay doo vol...
last call for passengers on flight...

DOUANE	CUSTOMS
CONTRÔLE DES PASSEPORTS	PASSPORT CONTROL
UE (Union Européenne)	EU (European Union)

With the single European market, EU (European Union) citizens are subject only to highly selective spot checks and they can go through the blue customs channel (unless they have goods to declare). There is no restriction by quantity or value on goods purchased by travellers in another EU country provided they are for their own personal use (guidelines have been published). If unsure, check with customs officials. Switzerland is not a member of the EU and you should check the current customs regulations.

I have nothing to declare
je n'ai rien à déclarer
zhuh nay ryañ a day-kla-ray

here is...	**my passport**	**my green card**
voici...	mon passeport	ma carte verte
vwa-see...	*moñ pass-por*	*ma kart vehrt*

do I have to pay duty on this?
je dois payer des droits de douane sur ça?
zhuh dwa pay-ay day drwa duh dwan soor sa

it's for my own personal use
c'est pour mon usage personnel
say poor moñ ooz-azh pehr-son-el

we're going to...	**the children are on this passport**
nous allons en...	les enfants sont sur ce passeport
nooz a-loñ oñ...	*layz oñ-foñ soñ soor suh pass-por*

I'm...	**British** (m/f)	**Australian** (m/f)
je suis...	britannique	australien(ne)
zhuh swee...	*bree-ta-neek*	*ohs-tra-lee-añ(en)*

ASKING THE WAY – questions

excuse me, please
excusez-moi, s'il vous plaît
eks-koo-zay-mwa seel voo play

where is the nearest...?
où est le/la ... le/la plus proche?
oo ay luh/la ... luh/la ploo prosh

how do I get to...?
pour aller à...?
poor al-ay a...

is this the right way to...?
c'est la bonne direction pour...?
say la bon dee-reks-yoñ poor...

the...
le/la...
luh/la...

can I walk there?
on peut y aller à pied?
oñ puh ee al-ay a pyay

is there a bus that goes there?
il y a un bus pour y aller?
eel ee a uñ boos poor ee al-ay

we're looking for...
nous cherchons...
noo shehr-shoñ...

we're lost
nous sommes perdus
noo som pehr-doo

can you show me on the map?
pouvez-vous me montrer sur la carte?
poo-vay-voo muh moñ-tray soor la kart

where is...?
où est...?
oo ay...

is it far?
c'est loin?
say lwañ

16

*It's no use being able to ask the way if you're not going to under-
stand the directions you get. We've tried to anticipate the likely
answers, so listen carefully for these key phrases.*

continuez tout droit
koñ-tee-noo-ay too drwa
keep going straight ahead

vous devez faire demi-tour
voo duh-vay fehr duh-mee-toor
you have to turn round

tournez...	**à droite**	**à gauche**
toor-nay...	*a drwat*	*a gohsh*
turn...	right	left

continuez...	**jusqu'à...**	**jusqu'à l'église**
koñ-tee-noo-ay...	*zhoos-ka...*	*zhoos-ka leg-leez*
keep going...	as far as...	as far as the church

traversez...	**la rue**	**la place**
tra-ver-say...	*la roo*	*la plass*
cross...	the street	the square

prenez...
pruh-nay...
take...

la première/deuxième à droite
la pruhm-yehr/duhz-yem a drwat
the first/second (road) on the right

c'est...
say...
it's...

après les feux
a-pray lay fuh
after the traffic lights

la direction de...
la dee-rek-syon duh...
the road to...

suivez les panneaux indicateurs en direction de...
swee-vay lay pan-oh añ-dee-ka-tuhr oñ dee-rek-syoñ duh...
follow the signs for...

BUS

L'ARRÊT DE BUS	BUS STOP

Coach travel in France is relatively cheap; ask for information about services and fares at the local bus station.

where is the bus station?
où est la gare routière?
oo ay la gar root-yehr

I want to go...
je voudrais aller...
zhuh voo-dray al-ay...

to the station
à la gare
a la gar

to the museum
au musée
oh moo-zay

to the city centre
au centre-ville
oh soñ-truh-veel

to Paris
à Paris
a pa-ree

is there a bus that goes there?
est-ce qu'il y a un bus pour y aller?
ess keel ee a uñ boos poor ee al-ay

which bus do I take for...?
quel bus dois-je prendre pour aller...?
kel boos dwa-zhuh proñdr poor al-ay...

where do I get the bus to...?
où est-ce qu'on prend le bus pour aller à...?
oo ess koñ proñ luh boos poor al-ay a...

how often are the buses?
les bus passent tous les combien?
lay boos pass too lay koñ-byañ

when is the last bus?
à quelle heure part le dernier bus?
a kel uhr par luh dehr-nyay boos

can you tell me when to get off?
pourriez-vous me dire quand descendre?
poo-ree-ay voo muh deer koñ day-soñdr

UNDERGROUND

MÉTRO	UNDERGROUND
ENTRÉE	ENTRANCE
SORTIE	EXIT

*In Paris the underground (**Metro**) is cheap and easy to use. You get a discount if you buy a book of ten tickets (**un carnet**). Children under 4 travel free, and for half-price between the ages of 4 and 10.*

Where is the metro station?
où est la station de métro?
oo ay la stass-yoñ duh met-roh

ten tickets, please
un carnet, s'il vous plaît
uñ kar-nay seel voo play

do you have an underground map?
est-ce que vous avez un plan du métro?
ess kuh vooz av-ay uñ ploñ <u>doo</u> met-roh

I want to go to...
je voudrais aller à...
zhuh voo-dray al-ay a...

can I go by underground?
est-ce que je peux y aller en métro?
ess kuh zhuh puh ee al-ay oñ met-roh

do I have to change?
est-ce qu'il faut changer?
ess keel foh shoñ-zhay

where?
où?
oo

which line is it for...?
c'est quelle ligne pour...?
say kel leen-yuh poor...

what is the next stop?
quel est le prochain arrêt?
kel ay luh pro-shañ ar-reh

which is the station for the Louvre?
c'est quelle station pour le Louvre?
say kel stass-yoñ poor luh loovr

TRAIN

GRANDES LIGNES	INTERCITY
TRAIN À SUPPLÉMENT	SUPPLEMENT PAYABLE
BILLETS ET RENSEIGNEMENTS	TICKETS AND INFORMATION
DÉPARTS	DEPARTURES
ARRIVÉES	ARRIVALS
QUAI	PLATFORM
BANLIEUE	LOCAL RAIL NETWORK

*France has an extensive rail network and trains are normally clean and on time. If you want to use the **TGV** service (high-speed train) you must book in advance. Fares may be higher at peak times, and some discounts are available only on 'blue days' – check the colour-coded **calendrier voyageurs**. Switzerland has an excellent rail service. You may be able to save on fares by buying a Swiss Pass (must be purchased before arriving in Switzerland).*

where is the station?
où est la gare?
oo ay la gar

to the station, please
à la gare, s'il vous plaît
a la gar seel voo play

a single to...
un aller simple pour...
uñ al-ay sañpl poor...

2 singles to...
deux allers simples pour...
duhz al-ay sañ-pluh poor...

a return to...
un aller retour pour...
uñ al-ay ruh-toor poor...

2 returns to...
deux aller retour pour...
duhz al-ay ruh-toor poor...

a child's return to...
un aller retour enfant pour...
uñ al-ay ruh-toor oñ-foñ poor...

1st class	**2nd class**	**smoking**	**non smoking**
première classe	seconde classe	fumeur	non fumeur
pruhm-yehr klass	*suh-goñd klass*	*foo-muhr*	*noñ foo-muhr*

do I have to pay a supplement?
je dois payer un supplément?
zhuh dwa pay-ay uñ soop-lay-moñ

is my pass valid on this train?
est-ce que ma carte est valable dans ce train?
ess kuh ma kart ay va-labl soor doñ suh trañ

I want to book...	**a seat**	**a couchette**
je voudrais réserver...	une place	une couchette
zhuh voo-dray ray-zehr-vay...	*oon plass*	*oon koo-shet*

do you have a train timetable?
est-ce que vous avez un horaire des trains?
ess kuh vooz av-ay un o-rehr day trañ

do I need to change?	**where?**
est-ce qu'il faut changer?	où?
ess keel foh shoñ-zhay	*oo*

which platform does it leave from?
il part de quel quai?
eel par duh kel kay

does the train to ... leave from this platform?
le train pour ... part de ce quai?
luh trañ poor ... par duh suh kay

is this the train for...?
c'est le train pour...?
say luh trañ poor...

where is the left-luggage?
où est la consigne?
oo ay la koñ-seen-yuh

is this seat free?
cette place est libre?
set plass ay leebr

TAXI

In France you must pick up a taxi from a taxi rank. A tip might be expected, whereas in Switzerland the tip is normally included in the fare.

to the airport, please
à l'aéroport, s'il vous plaît
a la-ehr-o-por seel voo play

to the station, please
à la gare, s'il vous plaît
a la gar seel voo play

to this address, please
à cette adresse, s'il vous plaît
a set a-dress seel voo play

how much will it cost?
combien ça coûtera?
koñ-byañ sa koo-tra

it's too much
c'est trop
say troh

how much is it to the centre?
combien ça coûte pour aller jusqu'au centre-ville?
koñ-byañ sa koot poor al-ay zhoo-skoh soñ-truh-veel

where can I get a taxi?
où est-ce que je peux prendre un taxi?
oo ess kuh zhuh puh proñdr uñ tak-see

please order me a taxi
pouvez-vous m'appeller un taxi?
poo-vay voo map-lay uñ tak-see

can I have a receipt?
est-ce que je peux avoir un reçu?
ess kuh zhuh puh av-war uñ ruh-soo

I've nothing smaller
je n'ai pas de monnaie
zhuh nay pa duh mon-ay

keep the change
gardez la monnaie
gar-day la mon-ay

In Switzerland lake steamers offer a pleasant alternative to other forms of travel. Fares are not cheap but the scenery is marvellous and children under 6 travel free.

1 ticket	**2 tickets**	**single**	**round trip**
un billet	deux billets	un aller simple	un aller retour
uñ bee-yay	*duh bee-yay*	*uñ al-ay sañpl*	*uñ al-ay ruh-toor*

is there a tourist ticket?
est-ce qu'il y a un billet touristique?
ess keel ee a uñ bee-yay too-rees-teek

are there any boat trips?
est-ce qu'il y a des excursions en bateau?
ess keel ee a dayz ek-skoors-yoñ oñ ba-toh

how long is the trip?
le voyage dure combien de temps?
luh vwa-yazh door koñ-byañ duh toñ

when is the next boat?
à quelle heure part le prochain bateau?
a kel uhr par luh pro-shañ ba-toh

when does the boat leave?
à quelle heure part le bateau?
a kel uhr par luh ba-toh

do you have a timetable?
est-ce que vous avez un horaire?
ess kuh vooz av-ay un o-rehr

can we eat on board?
on peut manger sur le bateau?
oñ puh moñ-zhay soor luh ba-toh

can we hire a boat?
on peut louer un bateau?
oñ puh loo-ay uñ ba-toh

CAR – driving/parking

TOUTES DIRECTIONS	ALL ROUTES
SORTIE	EXIT
AUTOROUTE	MOTORWAY
PÉAGE	TOLL
STATIONNEMENT INTERDIT	NO PARKING
CENTRE-VILLE	CITY CENTRE

*To drive in France and Switzerland visitors must be at least 18 years old and hold a valid UK licence. Seat belts are compulsory. Tolls are payable on most sections of French motorways (**autoroutes**) – you can pay by cash or credit card. Parking can be difficult, especially in Paris, but most towns do have pay and display systems (**horodateurs**). In Switzerland you must pay a tax to use the motorway; a tax sticker (**vignette**) can be bought at the border, or from Switzerland Tourism in advance of your trip.*

can I park here?
on peut se garer ici?
oñ puh suh gar-ay ee-see

where is the parking meter?
où est le parcmètre?
oo ay luh park-metr

where can I park?
où est-ce que je peux me garer?
oo ess kuh zhuh puh muh ga-ray

is there a car park?
est-ce qu'il y a un parking?
ess keel ee a uñ par-keeng

how long can I park here?
combien de temps peut-on stationner?
koñ-byañ duh toñ puht-oñ stass-yon-ay

we're going to...
nous allons à...
nooz a-loñ a...

what's the best route?
quelle est le meilleur itinéraire?
kel ay luh me-yuhr ee-tee-nay-rehr

is the pass open?
est-ce que le col est ouvert?
ess kuh luh kol ay oo-vehr

do I need snow chains?
est-ce qu'il faut des chaînes?
ess keel foh day shen

petrol station – CAR

SUPER	4 STAR
SANS PLOMB	UNLEADED
GAS-OIL	DIESEL

Petrol in France is expensive, especially at motorway service stations. Petrol stations in shopping complexes are often cheaper.

is there a petrol station near here?
est-ce qu'il y a une station-service près d'ici?
ess keel ee a <u>oon</u> stass-yoñ-sehr-vees pray dee-see

fill it up, please
le plein, s'il vous plaît
luh plañ seel voo play

200F-worth of unleaded petrol
deux cents francs d'essence sans plomb
duh soñ froñ de-soñss soñ ploñ

pump number...
pompe numéro...
poñp n<u>oo</u>-me-ro...

that's my car
voilà ma voiture
vwa-la ma vwa-t<u>oo</u>r

where is the air line?
où se trouve le compresseur?
oo suh troov luh koñ-pre-suhr

where is the water?
où se trouve l'eau?
oo suh troov loh

please check...
s'il vous plaît vérifiez...
seel voo play vay-reef-yay...

the tyre pressure
la pression des pneus
la press-yoñ day pnuh

the oil
l'huile
lweel

the water
l'eau
loh

quelle pompe?
kel poñp
which pump?

CAR – problems/breakdown

French and Swiss motorways have emergency telephones every 2 km. In the event of an accident or breakdown in France, use your hazard warning lights and/or a red warning triangle.

my car has broken down
ma voiture est en panne
ma vwa-toor ayt oñ pan

what do I do?
qu'est-ce que je dois faire?
kes kuh zhuh dwa fehr

I'm on my own (female)
je suis seule
zhuh swee suhl

I have children in the car
j'ai des enfants dans la voiture
zhay dayz oñ-foñ doñ la vwa-toor

where is the nearest garage?
où est le garage le plus proche?
oo ay luh ga-razh luh ploo prosh

is it serious?
c'est grave?
say grav

can you repair it?
est-ce que vous pouvez le réparer?
ess kuh voo poo-vay luh re-pa-ray

when will it be ready?
ça sera prêt quand?
sa suh-ra pray koñ

how much will it cost?
combien ça va coûter?
koñ-byañ sa va koo-tay

the car won't start
la voiture ne démarre pas
la vwa-toor nuh day-mar pa

I have a flat tyre
j'ai un pneu crevé
zhay uñ pnuh kruh-vay

the engine is overheating
le moteur chauffe
luh mo-tuhr shohf

the battery is flat
la batterie est à plat
la ba-tree ay a pla

have you got the parts?
vous avez les pièces de rechange?
vooz av-ay lay pyess duh ruh-shoñzh

it's not working
ça ne marche pas
sa nuh marsh pa

can you replace the windscreen?
pouvez-vous changer le pare-brise?
poo-vay voo shoñzhay luh par-breez

LOCATION DE VOITURES	CAR HIRE

All the main international car hire companies have offices in France. It may be cheaper to book in the UK before you leave. Drivers must be over 20 and have held a full driving licence for at least a year.

I would like to hire a car
je voudrais louer une voiture
zhuh voo-dray loo-ay oon vwa-toor

for one day
pour un jour
poor uñ zhoor

for ... days
pour ... jours
poor ... zhoor

I would like...
je voudrais...
zhuh voo-dray...

a large car
une grosse voiture
oon grohss vwa-toor

a small car
une petite voiture
oon puh-teet vwa-toor

a cheaper car
une voiture moins chère
oon vwa-toor mwañ shehr

an automatic
une automatique
oon oh-toh-ma-teek

is fully comprehensive insurance included?
est-ce que l'assurance tous-risques est comprise?
ess kuh l'ass-oo-roñss too reesk ay koñ-preez

what do we do if we break down?
qu'est-ce qu'il faut faire si la voiture tombe en panne?
kess keel foh fehr see la vwa-toor toñb oñ pan

when must I return the car by?
quand dois-je rapporter la voiture?
koñ dwazh ra-por-tay la vwa-toor

can you show me the controls?
pouvez-vous me montrer les commandes?
poo-vay voo muh moñ-tray lay ko-moñd

where are the documents?
où sont les papiers?
oo soñ lay pap-yay

SHOPPING – holiday

OUVERT	OPEN	**CAISSE**	CASH DESK
FERMÉ	CLOSED	**SOLDES**	SALE

Most shops are open from 9 or 10am until 6.30 or 7.30pm, and many close on Mondays. In rural areas they will also close for lunch, usually noon to 2pm. Most hypermarkets stay open till 9pm Mon-Sat. Some are also open on Sundays.

do you sell...?
est-ce que vous vendez...?
ess kuh voo voñ-day...

stamps
des timbres
day tañbr

batteries for this camera
des piles pour cet appareil
day peel poor set a-pa-ray

where can you buy...?
où est-ce qu'on peut acheter...?
oo ess koñ puh ash-tay...

stamps
des timbres
day tañbr

films
des pellicules
day pe-lee-kool

10 stamps
dix timbres
dee tañbr

for postcards
pour cartes postale
poor kart pos-tal

to Britain
pour la Grande-Bretagne
poor la groñd bruh-tan-yuh

a colour film
une pellicule couleur
oon pe-lee-kool koo-luhr

a tape for this video camera
une cassette vidéo pour ce caméscope
oon ka-set vee-day-oh poor suh ka-may-skop

I'm looking for a present
je cherche un cadeau
zhuh shehrsh uñ ka-doh

have you anything cheaper?
vous avez quelque chose de moins cher?
vooz av-ay kel-kuh shohz duh mwañ shehr

it's a gift
c'est un cadeau
sayt uñ ka-doh

could you wrap it up?
vous pouvez me l'envelopper?
voo poo-vay muh loñv-lop-ay

clothes – SHOPPING

WOMEN		MEN		SHOES			
UK	EU	UK	EU	UK	EU	UK	EU
8	36	36	46	2	35	8	42
10	38	38	48	3	36	9	43
12	40	40	50	4	37	10	44
14	42	42	52	5	38	11	45
16	44	44	54	6	39	12	46
18	46	46	56	7	41		

can I try this on?
est-ce que je peux l'essayer?
ess kuh zhuh puh le-say-yay

where are the changing rooms?
où sont les cabines d'essayage?
oo soñ lay ka-been deh-say-yazh

it's too big
c'est trop grand
say troh groñ

have you a smaller size?
vous l'avez en plus petit?
voo lav-ay oñ p<u>loo</u> puh-tee

it's too small
c'est trop petit
say troh puh-tee

have you a larger size?
vous l'avez en plus grand?
voo lav-ay oñ p<u>loo</u> groñ

it's too expensive
c'est trop cher
say troh shehr

I'm just looking
je regarde seulement
zhuh ruh-gard suhl-moñ

I'll take this one
je prends celui-ci
zhuh proñ suhl-wee-see

I take size 6 shoe
je fais du trente-neuf
zhuh fay d<u>oo</u> troñt-nuhf

quelle pointure faites-vous?	**ça vous va?**
kel pwañ-<u>toor</u> fet-voo	*sa voo va*
what shoe size are you?	**does it fit?**

SHOPPING – food

BOULANGERIE BAKER'S	**ÉPICERIE** GROCER'S
BOUCHERIE BUTCHER'S	**POISSONNERIE** FISHMONGER'S

The best place to buy fruit, vegetables and seasonal produce is in the local markets – most towns will have at least one market-day a week. Markets are usually open in the morning only.

where can I buy...?
où est-ce que je peux acheter...?
oo ess kuh zhuh puh ash-tay...

fruit	**bread**	**milk**
des fruits	du pain	du lait
day frwee	*doo pañ*	*doo lay*

where is the supermarket?
où est le supermarché?
oo ay luh soo-pehr-mar-shay

where is the baker's?
où est la boulangerie?
oo ay la boo-loñzh-ree

where is the market?
où est le marché?
oo ay luh mar-shay

which day is the market?
c'est quel jour, le marché?
say kel zhoor luh mar-shay

it's me next
c'est à moi
sayt a mwa

that's enough
ça suffit
sa soo-fee

a litre of...
un litre de...
uñ leetr duh...

milk	**beer**	**water**
lait	bière	eau
lay	*byehr*	*oh*

a bottle of...
une bouteille de...
oon boo-tay duh...

wine	**beer**	**water**
vin	bière	eau
vañ	*byehr*	*oh*

a can of... **coke**
une boîte de... coca
oon bwat duh... *ko-ka*

beer	**tonic water**
bière	tonic
byehr	*to-neek*

a packet of...
un paquet de...
uñ pa-kay duh...

biscuits	**sugar**
biscuits	sucre
bee-skwee	*sookr*

4 oz of... *(approx.)*
cent grammes de...
soñ gram duh...

cheese
fromage
fro-mazh

ham
jambon
zhoñ-boñ

half a pound of... *(approx.)*
250 grammes de...
duh soñ sañ-koñt gram duh...

butter
beurre
buhr

mince
viande hachée
vyoñd ash-ay

a kilo of...
un kilo de...
uñ kee-loh duh...

potatoes
pommes de terre
pom duh ter

apples
pommes
pom

8 slices of...
huit tranches de...
wee troñsh duh...

ham
jambon
joñ-boñ

salami
saucisson
soh-see-soñ

a loaf of bread
un pain
uñ pañ

a baguette
une baguette
oon ba-get

half a dozen eggs
six œufs
seez uh

a tin of...
une boîte de...
oon bwat duh...

tomatoes
tomates
to-mat

peas
petits pois
puh-tee pwa

a jar of...
un pot de...
uñ poh duh...

jam
confiture
koñ-fee-toor

honey
miel
myell

vous désirez?
voo day-zee-ray
can I help you?

ce sera tout?
suh suh-ra too
is that everything?

vous voulez un sac?
voo voo-lay uñ sak
would you like a bag?

SIGHTSEEING

LE SYNDICAT D'INITIATIVE   TOURIST OFFICE

Tourist offices will be able to give you information on local attractions. French national museums are usually closed on Tuesday; under-18s get in free, and there are concessions for 18-25s and over-60s. Local museums are closed on Monday; entrance is usually free on Sundays, and for those under 7 and over 60.

where is the tourist office?
où est le syndicat d'initiative?
oo ay luh sañ-dee-ka dee-nee-sya-teev

do you have a town guide?
vous avez un plan de la ville?
vooz av-ay uñ ploñ duh la veel

we want to visit...
nous voulons visiter...
noo voo-loñ vee-zee-tay...

have you any leaflets?
vous avez des brochures?
vooz av-ay day bro-shoor

is it open to the public?
est-ce que c'est ouvert au public?
ess kuh say oo-vehr oh poob-leek

are there any sightseeing tours?
est-ce qu'il y a des visites guidées?
ess keel ee a day vee-zeet gee-day

when does it leave?
à quelle heure part-il?
a kel uhr part-eel

where does it leave from?
il part d'où?
eel par doo

how much is it to get in?
c'est combien l'entrée?
say koñ-byañ loñ-tray

are there reductions for...?
est-ce qu'il y a des réductions pour...?
ess keel ee a day ray-dooks-yoñ poor...

students
les étudiants
layz ay-tood-yoñ

children
les enfants
layz oñ-foñ

senior citizens
les retraités
lay ruh-tret-ay

BEACH

BAIGNADE INTERDITE	NO SWIMMING
INTERDICTION DE PLONGER	NO DIVING

Most beaches in France are open to the public, and are often patrolled by lifeguards during the tourist season. A green flag means it is safe to swim; orange means swimming is unsafe but lifeguards are present; red means it is too dangerous to go swimming. There are no restrictions on going topless.

can you recommend a quiet beach?
est-ce que vous connaissez une plage tranquille?
ess kuh.voo ko-ness-ay <u>oo</u>n plazh troñ-keel

is there a swimming pool?
est-ce qu'il y a une piscine?
ess keel ee a <u>oo</u>n pee-seen

can we swim in the river?
on peut nager dans la rivière?
oñ puh na-zhay doñ la reev-yehr

is the water clean?
est-ce que l'eau est propre?
ess kuh loh ay propr

is the water deep?
est-ce que l'eau est profonde?
ess kuh loh ay pro-foñd

is the water cold?
est-ce que l'eau est froide?
ess kuh loh ay frwad

is it dangerous?
est-ce que c'est dangereux?
ess kuh say doñ-zhuh-ruh

are there currents?
est-ce qu'il y a des courants?
ess keel ee a day koo-roñ

where can we...?
où est-ce qu'on peut faire...?
oo ess koñ puh fehr...

surf
du surf
d<u>oo</u> suhrf

waterski
du ski nautique
d<u>oo</u> skee noh-teek

can we hire...?
est-ce qu'on peut louer...?
ess koñ puh loo-ay...

a sunshade
un parasol
uñ pa-ra-sol

a deck chair
un transat
uñ troñ-za

SPORT

French tourist offices provide information on sports facilities in the local area.

where can we...?
où est-ce qu'on peut...?
oo ess koñ puh...

play tennis
jouer au tennis
zhway oh ten-ees

play golf
jouer au golf
zhway oh golf

go riding
faire du cheval
fehr <u>doo</u> shuh-val

go fishing
pêcher
pesh-ay

how much is it...?
c'est combien...?
say koñ-byañ...

per hour
l'heure
luhr

per day
la journée
la zhoor-nay

can I hire...?
je peux louer...?
zhuh puh loo-ay...

rackets
des raquettes
day ra-ket

golf-clubs
des clubs de golf
day klub duh golf

how do I book a court?
comment dois-je faire pour réserver un court?
ko-moñ dwazh fehr poor ray-zehr-vay uñ koor

do I need a fishing permit?
est-ce qu'il faut avoir un permis de pêche?
ess keel foh av-war uñ per-mee duh pesh

is there a football match?
est-ce qu'il y a un match de football?
ess keel ee a uñ match duh foot-bol

do I need walking boots?
est-ce qu'il faut des chaussures de marche?
ess keel foh day sho-<u>soor</u> duh marsh

where is there a sports shop?
où est-ce qu'il y a un magasin de sports?
oo ess keel ee a uñ ma-ga-zañ duh spor

I'd like to hire skis
je voudrais louer des skis
zhuh voo-dray loo-ay day skee

how much is a pass?
c'est combien le forfait?
say koñ-byañ luh for-fay

I'm a beginner
je suis débutant
zhuh swee day-boo-toñ

is there a map of the ski runs?
il y a une carte des pistes?
eel ee a oon kart day peest

which is an easy run?
laquelle de ces pistes est facile?
la-kel duh ses peest ay fa-seel

my skis are...
mes skis sont...
may skee soñ...

too long
trop longs
troh loñ

too short
trop courts
troh koor

my bindings...
mes fixations...
may feek-sass-yoñ...

are too loose
ne sont pas assez serrés
nuh soñ pa as-ay ser-ay

are too tight
sont trop serrées
soñ troh ser-ay

can you adjust my bindings?
pourriez-vous régler mes fixations?
poo-ree-ay voo reg-lay may feek-sass-yoñ

where can we go cross-country skiing?
où est-ce qu'on peut faire du ski de fond?
oo ess koñ puh fehr doo skee duh foñ

quelle longueur de skis voulez-vous?
kel loñ-guhr duh skee voo-lay voo
what length skis do you want?

quelle pointure faites-vous?
kel pwañ-toor fet voo
what is your shoe size?

NIGHTLIFE – popular

what is there to do at night?
qu'est-ce qu'on peut faire le soir?
kess koñ puh fehr luh swar

which is a good bar?
vous connaissez un bon bar?
voo ko-ness-ay uñ boñ bar

is it expensive?
c'est cher?
say shehr

which is a good disco?
vous connaissez une bonne discothèque?
voo ko-ness-ay oon bon dees-ko-tek

where can we hear live music?
où est-ce qu'on peut écouter de la musique live?
oo ess koñ puh ay-koo-tay duh la moo-seek laeev

where do local people go at night?
où est-ce que les gens du coin vont le soir?
oo ess kuh lay zhoñ doo kwañ voñ luh swar

is it a safe area?
ce n'est pas un quartier dangereux?
suh nay pa uñ kart-yay doñ-zhuh-ruh

are there any concerts?
est qu'il y a de bons concerts?
ess keel ee a duh boñ koñ-sehr

is there a guide to what's on?
est-ce qu'il y a un guide des spectacles et des sorties?
ess keel ee a uñ geed day spek-takl ay day sor-tee

---

tu veux danser?
too vuh doñ-say
do you want to dance?

je m'appelle...
zhuh ma-pel...
my name is...

comment t'appelles-tu?
ko-moñ ta-pel too
what's your name?

*The easiest way to find out what's on in Paris is to buy one of the publications that lists cultural events (such as **Pariscope**, available from newsstands). Tickets can be bought at the door, or in advance at **FNAC** (a chain store).*

is there a list of cultural events?
est-ce qu'il y a une liste des événements culturels?
ess keel ee a <u>oon</u> leest dayz ay-ven-moñ <u>kool</u>-<u>too</u>-rel

are there any local festivals?
est-ce qu'il y a des fêtes dans la région?
ess keel ee a day fet doñ la rezh-yon

we'd like to go...
nous voudrions aller...
noo voo-dree-oñ al-ay...

to the theatre
au théâtre
oh tay-atr

to the opera
à l'opéra
a lo-pe-ra

to the ballet
au ballet
oh bal-ay

to a concert
à un concert
a uñ koñ-sehr

what's on?
quels sont les spectacles à l'affiche?
kel soñ lay spek-takl a la-feesh

do I need to book?
est-ce qu'il faut réserver?
ess keel foh ray-zehr-vay

how much are the tickets?
c'est combien l'entrée?
say koñ-byañ loñ-tray

2 tickets...
deux billets...
duh bee-yay...

for tonight
pour ce soir
poor suh swar

for tomorrow night
pour demain soir
poor duh-mañ swar

for 5th August
le cinq août
luh sañk oot

when does the performance end?
quand finit la représentation?
koñ fee-nee la ruh-pray-zoñ-tass-yoñ

HOTEL

Offices de Tourisme and *Syndicats d'Initiative* can give you information on hotels and other kinds of accommodation, including *chambres d'hôte* (bed and breakfast).

have you a room for tonight?
vous avez une chambre pour ce soir?
vooz av-ay <u>oo</u>n shoñbr poor se swar

single	**double**	**for a family**
pour une personne	pour deux personnes	pour une famille
poor <u>oo</u>n pehr-son	*poor duh pehr-son*	*poor <u>oo</u>n fa-mee*
	with a bath	**with a shower**
	avec bain	avec douche
	a-vek bañ	*a-vek doosh*

how much is it per night?
c'est combien par nuit?
say koñ-byañ par nwee

is breakfast included?
le petit déjeuner est compris?
luh puh-tee day-zhuh-nay ay koñ-pree

I booked a room
j'ai réservé une chambre
zhay ray-zehr-vay <u>oo</u>n shoñbr

my name is...
je m'appelle...
zhuh ma-pel...

I'd like to see the room
je voudrais voir la chambre
zhuh voo-dray vwar la shoñbr

have you anything less expensive?
vous avez quelque chose de moins cher?
vooz av-ay kel-kuh shohz duh mwañ shehr

can I leave this in the safe?
je peux laisser cela dans le coffre?
zhuh puh less-ay suh-la doñ luh koffr

can I have my key, please
ma clé, s'il vous plaît
ma klay seel voo play

are there any messages for me?
il y a des messages pour moi?
eel ee a day muh-sazh poor mwa

come in!
entrez!
oñ-tray

please come back later
s'il vous plaît, revenez plus tard
seel voo play ruh-vuh-nay ploo tar

I'd like breakfast in my room
je voudrais le petit-déjeuner dans ma chambre
zhuh voo-dray luh puh-tee-day-zhuh-nay doñ ma shoñbr

please bring...
pouvez-vous m'apporter...
poo-vay voo ma-por-tay...

toilet paper
du papier hygiénique
doo pap-yay ee-zhyen-eek

soap
du savon
doo sa-voñ

clean towels
des serviettes propres
day sehr-vyet propr

a glass
un verre
uñ vehr

please clean...
pouvez-vous nettoyer...
poo-vay voo ne-twa-yay...

my room
ma chambre
ma shoñbr

the bath
la baignoire
la ben-war

please call me...
pouvez-vous m'appeler...
poo-vay voo map-lay...

at 7 o'clock
à sept heures
a set uhr

is there a laundry service?
vous avez un service de blanchisserie?
vooz av-ay uñ sehr-veess duh bloñ-sheess-ree

I'm leaving tomorrow
je pars demain
zhuh par duh-mañ

could you prepare the bill?
pouvez-vous préparer la note?
poo-vay-voo pray-pa-ray la not

SELF-CATERING

The voltage in France and Switzerland is 220, and most plugs are two-pin, so if you plan to take any electrical appliances with you make sure you have an adaptor.

which is the key for this door?
quelle est la clé de cette porte?
kel ay la klay duh set port

please show us how this works
montrez-nous comment ça marche, s'il vous plaît
moñ-tray-noo ko-moñ sa marsh seel voo play

how does ... work?	**the cooker**	**the heating**
comment fonctionne...?	la cuisinière	le chauffage
ko-moñ foñks-yon...	*la kwee-zeen-yehr*	*luh shoh-fazh*
	the washing machine	**the dryer**
	la machine à laver	le séchoir
	la ma-sheen a lav-ay	*luh sesh-war*

who do I contact if there are any problems?
qui faut-il contacter s'il y a un problème?
kee foht-eel kon-tak-tay seel ee a uñ prob-lem

we need extra...	**cutlery**	**sheets**
il faut encore des...	couverts	draps
eel foh oñ-kor day...	*koo-vehr*	*dra*

the gas has run out
il n'y a plus de gaz
eel nee a ploo duh gaz

what do I do?
qu'est-ce qu'il faut faire?
kes keel foh fehr

where are the fuses?
où sont les plombs?
oo soñ lay ploñ

where do I put the rubbish?
où est-ce que je dois mettre la poubelle?
oo ess kuh zhuh dwa metr la poo-bel

CAMPING & CARAVANNING

*Both France and Switzerland have excellent campsites.
Regulations regarding off-site camping vary and you can avoid
problems by sticking to official sites. In Switzerland the speed limit
for a car towing a caravan is 50 kph in built-up areas and 80 kph
on other roads. Speed limits in France vary according to weather
conditions, the weight of the trailer, etc.*

we're looking for a campsite
nous cherchons un camping
noo shehr-shoñ uñ kam-peeng

have you a list of campsites?
avez-vous un guide des campings?
av-ay-voo uñ geed day koñ-peeng

where is the campsite?
où est le camping?
oo ay luh koñ-peeng

have you any vacancies?
il vous reste des places?
eel voo rest day plass

how much is it per night?
c'est combien la nuit?
say koñ-byañ la nwee

we'd like to stay for ... nights
nous voudrions rester ... nuits
noo voo-dree-oñ res-tay ... nwee

is the campsite near the beach?
est-ce que le camping est près de la plage?
ess kuh luh koñ-peeng ay pray duh la plazh

can we have a more sheltered site?
est-ce que nous pouvons avoir un emplacement plus abrité?
ess kuh noo poo-voñ av-war un oñ-plass-moñ plooz ab-ree-tay

this site is very muddy
ce terrain est très boueux
suh te-rañ ay tray boo-uh

is there another site?
il y a un autre emplacement?
eel ee a un ohtr oñ-plass-moñ

is there a shop on the site?
il y a un magasin dans le camping?
eel ee a uñ ma-ga-zañ doñ luh koñ-peeng

can we camp here?
est-ce qu'on peut camper ici?
ess koñ puh koñ-pay ee-see

can we park our caravan here?
est-ce que nous pouvons mettre notre caravane ici?
ess kuh noo poo-voñ metr notr ka-ra-van ee-see

CHILDREN

In France children under 10 must travel in the back of the car using a child safety seat or restraint. In Switzerland children under 12 must sit in the back.

a child's ticket
un billet tarif enfant
uñ bee-yay ta-reef oñ-foñ

he/she is ... years old
il/elle a ... ans
eel/el a ... oñ

is there a reduction for children?
est-ce qu'il y a une réduction pour les enfants?
ess keel ee a <u>oo</u>n ray-d<u>oo</u>ks-yoñ poor layz oñ-foñ

do you have a children's menu?
est-ce que vous avez un menu pour les enfants?
ess kuh vooz av-ay uñ muh-n<u>oo</u> poor layz oñ-foñ

do you have...?
est-ce que vous avez...?
ess kuh vooz av-ay...

a high chair
une chaise de bébé
<u>oo</u>n shehz duh bay-bay

a cot
un lit d'enfant
uñ lee doñ-foñ

is it ok to take children?
on peut y aller avec des enfants?
oñ puh ee al-ay a-vek dayz oñ-foñ

what is there for children to do?
quelles sont les activités prévues pour les enfants?
kel soñ layz ak-tee-vee-tay pray-v<u>oo</u> poor layz oñ-foñ

is it safe for children?
c'est sans danger pour les enfants?
say soñ doñ-zhay poor layz oñ-foñ

is it dangerous?
est-ce que c'est dangereux?
ess kuh say doñ-zhuh-ruh

I have two children
j'ai deux enfants
zhay duhz oñ-foñ

he/she is 10 years old
il/elle a dix ans
eel/el a deez oñ

do you have children?
est-ce que vous avez des enfants?
ess kuh vooz av-ay dayz oñ-foñ

SPECIAL NEEDS

Provision for disabled travellers in France is improving, although facilities are still patchy. The French Tourist Office has lists of hotels which offer facilities for disabled guests, but it's always advisable to contact hotels yourself to check that your needs can be met.

is it possible to visit ... with a wheelchair?
est-ce qu'on peut visiter ... en fauteuil roulant?
ess koñ puh vee-zee-tay ... oñ foh-tuhy roo-loñ

do you have toilets for the disabled?
est-ce que vous avez des toilettes pour handicapés?
ess kuh vooz av-ay day twa-let poor oñ-dee-ka-pay

I need a bedroom on the ground floor
j'ai besoin d'une chambre au rez-de-chaussée
zhay buhz-wañ doon shoñbr oh ray duh shoh-say

is there a lift?
est-ce qu'il y a un ascenseur?
ess keel ee a uñ ass-oñ-suhr

where is the lift?
où est l'ascenseur?
oo ay lass-oñ-suhr

I can't walk far
je ne peux pas aller très loin à pied
zhuh nuh puh paz al-ay tray lwañ a pyay

are there many steps?
il y a beaucoup de marches?
eel ee a boh-koo duh marsh

is there an entrance for wheelchairs?
est-ce qu'il y a une entrée pour les fauteuils roulants?
ess keel ee a oon oñ-tray poor lay foh-tuhy roo-loñ

can I travel on this train with a wheelchair?
est-ce que je peux prendre ce train avec un fauteuil roulant?
ess kuh zhuh puh proñdr suh trañ a-vek oñ foh-tuhy roo-loñ

is there a reduction for the disabled?
est-ce qu'il y a une réduction pour les handicapés?
ess keel ee a oon ray-dooks-yoñ poor lay oñ-dee-kap-ay

EXCHANGE VISITORS

These phrases are intended for families hosting French-speaking visitors. We have used the familiar tu form.

what would you like for breakfast?
qu'est-ce que tu veux manger pour le petit-déjeuner?
kess kuh too vuh moñ-zhay poor luh puh-tee day-zhuh-nay

what would you like to eat/drink?
qu'est-ce que tu veux manger/boire?
kess kuh too vuh moñ-zhay/bwar

did you sleep well?
tu as bien dormi?
too a byañ dor-mee

would you like to take a shower?
tu veux prendre une douche?
too vuh proñdr oon doosh

what would you like to do today?
qu'est-ce que tu veux faire aujourd'hui?
kess kuh too vuh fehr oh-zhoor-dwee

would you like to go shopping?
tu veux aller faire du shopping?
too vuh al-ay fehr doo shop-eeng

I will pick you up at...
je passerai te prendre à...
zhuh pass-ray tuh proñdr a...

did you enjoy yourself?
est-ce que tu t'es bien amusé?
ess kuh too tay byan a-moo-zay

take care
fais attention à toi
fayz a-toñss-yon a twa

please be back by...
tâche de rentrer avant...
tash duh roñ-tray a-voñ...

we'll be in bed when you get back
nous serons au lit lorsque tu rentreras
noo suh-roñ oh lee lors-kuh too roñ-truh-ra

44

EXCHANGE VISITORS

These phrases are intended for those people staying with French-speaking families.

I like...
j'aime bien...
zhem byañ...

I don't like...
je n'aime pas...
zhuh nem pa...

that was delicious
c'était délicieux
se-tay day-lee-syuh

thank you very much
merci beaucoup
mehr-see boh-koo

may I...?
est-ce que je peux...?
ess kuh zhuh puh...

phone home
téléphoner chez moi
te-le-foh-nay shay mwa

make a local call
passer un appel local
pass-ay un a-pel lo-kal

can you take me by car?
est-ce que vous pouvez m'emmener en voiture?
ess kuh voo poo-vay moñm-nay oñ vwa-toor

can I borrow...?
je peux emprunter...?
zhuh puh oñ-pruñ-tay...

an iron
un fer à repasser
uñ fehr a ruh-pass-ay

a hairdryer
un sèche-cheveux
uñ sesh-shuh-vuh

what time do I have to get up?
à quelle heure faut-il que je me lève?
a kel uhr foht-eel kuh zhuh muh lev

please would you call me at...?
pouvez-vous m'appeler à ... heures, s'il vous plaît?
poo-vay voo map-lay a ... uhr seel voo play

how long are you staying?
combien de temps restez-vous?
koñ-byañ duh toñ res-tay-voo

I'm leaving in a week
je m'en vais dans une semaine
zhuh moñ vay doñz oon suh-men

thanks for everything
merci pour tout
mehr-see poor too

I've had a great time
j'ai passé des moments formidables
zhay pass-ay day mo-moñ for-mee-dabl

PROBLEMS

can you help me?
pouvez-vous m'aider?
poo-vay voo may-day

I don't speak French
je ne parle pas français
zhuh nuh parl pa froñ-say

do you speak English?
parlez-vous anglais?
par-lay voo oñ-glay

does anyone speak English?
il y a quelqu'un qui parle anglais?
eel ee a kel-kuñ kee parl oñ-glay

I'm lost
je me suis perdu
zhuh muh swee pehr-<u>doo</u>

how do I get to...?
pour aller à...?
poor al-ay a...

I'm late
je suis en retard
zhuh swee oñ ruh-tar

I need to get to...
je dois aller à...
zhuh dwa al-ay a...

I've missed...
j'ai manqué...
zhay moñ-kay...

my plane
mon avion
mon av-yon

my connection
ma correspondance
ma ko-res-poñ-doñss

I've lost...
j'ai perdu...
zhay pehr-<u>doo</u>...

my money
mon argent
mon ar-zhoñ

my passport
mon passeport
moñ pass-por

my camera
mon appareil-photo
mon a-pa-ray foh-toh

my keys
mes clés
may klay

my luggage has not arrived
mes bagages ne sont pas arrivés
may ba-gazh nuh soñ pa a-ree-vay

I've left my bag in...
j'ai laissé mon sac dans...
zhay less-ay moñ sak doñ...

I have no money
je n'ai pas d'argent
zhuh nay pa dar-zhoñ

leave me alone!
laissez-moi tranquille!
less-ay-mwa troñ-keel

go away!
allez-vous-en!
al-ay vooz-oñ

COMPLAINTS

light
la lumière
la loom-yehr

the air conditioning
la climatisation
la klee-ma-tee-zas-yoñ

...doesn't work
...ne marche pas
...nuh marsh pa

the room is dirty
la chambre est sale
la shoñbr ay sal

the bath is dirty
la baignoire est sale
la ben-war ay sal

there is no...
il n'y a pas...
eel nee a pa...

hot water
d'eau chaude
doh shohd

toilet paper
de papier hygiénique
duh pap-yay ee-zhyen-eek

it is too noisy
il y a trop de bruit
eel ee a troh duh brwee

the room is too small
la chambre est trop petite
la shoñbr ay troh puh-teet

this isn't what I ordered
ce n'est pas ce que j'ai commandé
suh nay pa suh kuh zhay ko-moñ-day

I want to complain
je veux faire une réclamation
zhuh vuh fehr oon ray-kla-mass-yoñ

I want a refund
je veux être remboursé
zhuh vuh etr roñ-boor-say

we've been waiting for a very long time
nous attendons depuis très longtemps
nooz a-toñ-doñ duh-pwee tray loñ-toñ

there is a mistake
il y a une erreur
eel ee a oon e-ruhr

this is broken
c'est cassé
say kass-ay

can you repair it?
pouvez-vous le réparer?
poo-vay-voo luh ray-pa-ray

EMERGENCIES

POLICE	POLICE
POMPIERS	FIRE BRIGADE
URGENCES	ACCIDENT AND EMERGENCY DEPARTMENT

	France	Switzerland
POLICE	*17*	*117*
AMBULANCE (SAMU)	*15*	*118*
FIRE	*18*	*118*

help!
au secours!
oh suh-koor

can you help me?
pouvez-vous m'aider?
poo-vay-voo may-day

there's been an accident
il y a eu un accident
eel ee a <u>oo</u> un ak-see-doñ

someone is injured
il y a un blessé
eel ee a uñ bless-ay

call...
appelez...
ap-lay...

the police
la police
la po-leess

an ambulance
une ambulance
oon oñ-b<u>oo</u>-loñss

the fire brigade
les pompiers
lay poñ-pyay

he was driving too fast
il allait trop vite
eel al-ay troh veet

I need a report for my insurance
il me faut un constat pour mon assurance
eel muh foh uñ koñ-sta poor mon ass-<u>oo</u>-roñss

I've been robbed
on m'a volé
oñ ma vol-ay

my car has been broken into
on a forcé ma voiture
on a for-say ma vwa-toor

my car has been stolen
on m'a volé ma voiture
oñ ma vol-ay ma vwa-toor

I've been attacked
on m'a attaqué
oñ ma a-tak-ay

I've been raped
on m'a violée
oñ ma vyol-ay

that man keeps following me
cet homme me suit
set om muh swee

how much is the fine?
c'est combien l'amende?
say koñ-byañ lam-oñd

can I pay at the police station?
est-ce que je peux payer au commissariat de police?
ess kuh zhuh puh pay-ay oh ko-mee-sar-ya duh po-leess

I would like to phone my embassy
je voudrais appeler mon ambassade
zhuh voo-dray ap-lay mon oñ-ba-sad

where is the British consulate?
où est le consulat britannique?
oo ay luh koñ-soo-la bree-ta-neek

I have no money
je n'ai pas d'argent
zhuh nay pa dar-zhoñ

nous arrivons
nooz a-ree-voñ
we're on our way

HEALTH

PHARMACIE	PHARMACY
HÔPITAL	HOSPITAL
URGENCES	ACCIDENT AND EMERGENCY DEPARTMENT

All EU citizens are entitled to emergency care in France, but you will have to pay for treatment and claim reimbursement using your E111 form (which must be completed and stamped at a post office in the UK before your trip). You are not entitled to non-emergency treatment, and it is therefore advisable to take out a health insurance policy. If you are travelling in Switzerland, which is not a member of the EU and has no national health service, it is essential to have private health insurance.

have you something for...?
avez-vous quelque chose contre...?
av-ay-voo kel-kuh shohz koñtr...

flu
la grippe
la greep

diarrhoea
la diarrhée
la dee-ar-ay

is it safe to give children?
c'est sans danger pour les enfants?
say soñ doñ-zhay poor layz oñ-foñ

I don't feel well
je me sens mal
zhuh muh soñ mal

I need a doctor
j'ai besoin d'un médecin
zhay buhz-woñ duñ mayd-sañ

my son/daughter is ill
mon fils/ma fille est malade
moñ feess/ma fee ay ma-lad

he/she has a temperature
il/elle a de la fièvre
eel/el a duh la fyehvr

I'm taking these drugs
je prends ces médicaments
zhuh proñ say may-dee-ka-moñ

I have high blood pressure
j'ai de la tension
zhay duh la toñss-yoñ

I'm pregnant
je suis enceinte
zhuh sweez oñ-sañt

I'm on the pill
je prends la pilule
zhuh proñ la pee-lool

I'm allergic to penicillin
je suis allergique à la penicilline
zhuh sweez a-lehr-zheek a la pe-nee-see-leen

my blood group is...
mon groupe sanguin est...
moñ groop soñ-gañ ay...

I'm breastfeeding
j'allaite mon enfant
zha-let mon oñ-foñ

can I take it?
est-ce que je peux en prendre?
ess kuh zhuh puh oñ proñdr

will he/she have to go to hospital?
est-ce qu'il/qu'elle devra aller à l'hôpital?
ess keel/kel duhv-ra al-ay a lop-ee-tal

I need to go to casualty
je dois aller aux urgences
zhuh dwa al-ay ohz <u>oor</u>-zhoñss

where is the hospital?
où est l'hôpital?
oo ay lop-ee-tal

when are visiting hours?
quelles sont les heures de visite?
kel soñ layz uhr duh vee-zeet

which ward?
quel service?
kel sehr-veess

I need to see a dentist
j'ai besoin de voir un dentiste
zhay buhz-wañ duh vwar uñ doñ-teest

I have toothache
j'ai mal aux dents
zhay mal oh doñ

the filling has come out
le plombage est parti
luh ploñ-bazh ay par-tee

it hurts
ça me fait mal
sa muh fay mal

my dentures are broken
mon dentier est cassé
moñ doñt-yay ay kass-ay

can you repair them?
vous pouvez le réparer?
voo poo-vay luh ray-par-ay

I have an abscess
j'ai un abcès
zhay un ab-seh

BUSINESS

Office hours vary, but in France offices are usually open 9am to noon and 2-5pm Mon-Fri, and in Switzerland the hours are the same except they open one hour earlier in the morning.

I'm...
je suis...
zhuh swee...

here's my card
voici ma carte de visite
vwa-see ma kart duh vee-zeet

I'm from Jones Ltd
je suis de la compagnie Jones
zhuh swee duh la koñ-pan-yee Jones

I'd like to arrange a meeting with Mr/Ms...
j'aimerais arranger une entrevue avec Monsieur/Madame...
zhe-muh-ray a-roñ-zhay oon oñ-truh-voo a-vek muh-syuh/ma-dam...

on 4 May at 11 o'clock
pour le quatre mai à onze heures
poor luh katr may a oñz uhr

can we meet at a restaurant?
est-ce que nous pouvons nous rencontrer dans un restaurant?
ess kuh noo poo-voñ noo roñ-koñ-tray doñz uñ res-toh-roñ

I will confirm by fax
je confirmerai par fax
zhuh koñ-feer-muh-ray par faks

I'm staying at Hotel...
je suis à l'Hôtel...
zhuh swee a loh-tel...

how do I get to your office?
comment se rend-on à votre bureau?
ko-moñ suh roñ-toñ a votr boo-roh

here is some information about my company
voici de la documentation concernant ma compagnie
vwa-see duh la do-koo-moñ-tass-yoñ koñ-sehr-noñ ma koñ-pan-yee

I have an appointment with...
j'ai rendez-vous avec...
zhay roñ-day-voo a-vek...

at ... o'clock
à ... heures
a ... uhr

I'm delighted to meet you
je suis enchanté de faire votre connaissance
zhuh sweez oñ-shañ-tay duh fehr votr ko-nay-soñss

my French isn't very good
mon français n'est pas très bon
moñ froñ-say nay pa tray boñ

what is the name of the managing director?
comment s'appelle le directeur?
ko-moñ sa-pel luh dee-rek-tuhr

I would like some information about the company
je voudrais des renseignements sur l'entreprise
zhuh voo-dray day roñ-sen-yuh-moñ soor loñ-truh-preez

do you have a press office?
est-ce que vous avez un service de presse?
ess kuh vooz av-ay uñ sehr-veess duh press

I need an interpreter
j'ai besoin d'un interprète
zhay buhz-wañ dun añ-tehr-pret

can you photocopy this for me?
pouvez-vous me photocopier ça?
poo-vay voo muh fo-to-kop-yay sa

is there a business centre?
est-ce qu'il y a un service de secrétariat?
ess keel ee a uñ sehr-veess duh suh-kray-ta-ree-a

---

est-ce que vous avez rendez-vous?
ess kuh vooz a-vay roñ-day-voo
do you have an appointment?

PHONING

Most payphones in France and Switzerland now take phonecards (**télécartes**), which you can buy at tobacconists, newsagents and post offices. In France the cheap rate for phone calls applies on weekdays between 10.30pm and 8am, and on weekends starting 2pm on Saturday. To call the UK from France or Switzerland dial 00 44.

a phonecard
une télécarte
oon te-le-kart

I want to make a phone call
je voudrais téléphoner
zhuh voo-dray te-le-foh-nay

I wish to make a reverse charge call
je voudrais téléphoner en PCV
zhuh voo-dray te-le-foh-nay oñ pe-se-vay

can I speak to...?
je peux parler à...
zhuh puh par-lay a...

this is...
c'est...
say...

Monsieur Citron please
Monsieur Citron s'il vous plaît
muh-syuh see-troñ seel voo play

I'll call back later
je vais rappeler plus tard
zhuh vay rap-lay ploo tar

can you give me an outside line, please
est-ce que je peux avoir la ligne, s'il vous plaît?
ess kuh zhuh puh av-war la leen-yuh seel voo play

allô?
a-loh
hello?

c'est de la part de qui?
say duh la par duh kee
who is calling?

c'est occupé
say o-koo-pay
it's engaged

pouvez-vous rappeler plus tard?
poo-vay voo rap-lay ploo tar
please try again later

I want to send a fax
je voudrais envoyer un fax
zhuh voo-dray oñ-vwa-yay uñ faks

do you have a fax?
vous avez un fax?
vooz av-ay uñ faks

what's your fax number?
quel est votre numéro de fax?
kel ay votr noo-me-ro duh faks

please resend your fax
veuillez nous renvoyer votre fax
vuh-yay noo roñ-vwa-yay votr faks

I can't read it
je ne peux pas le lire
zhuh nuh puh pa luh leer

your fax is engaged
votre fax est occupé
votr faks ay o-koo-pay

can I send a fax from here?
est-ce que je peux envoyer un fax d'ici?
ess kuh zhuh puh oñ-vwa-yay uñ faks dee-see

did you get my fax?
est-ce que vous avez reçu mon fax?
ess kuh vooz av-ay ruh-soo moñ faks

I want to send an e-mail
je voudrais envoyer un e-mail
zhuh voo-dray oñ-vwa-yay uñ ee-mel

what's your e-mail address?
quelle est votre addresse électronique?
kel ay votr a-dress e-lek-tro-neek

did you get my e-mail?
est-ce que vous avez reçu mon e-mail?
ess kuh vooz av-ay ruh-soo mon ee-mel

NUMBERS

0	**zéro**	*ze-ro*
1	**un**	*uñ*
2	**deux**	*duh*
3	**trois**	*trwa*
4	**quatre**	*katr*
5	**cinq**	*sañk*
6	**six**	*seess*
7	**sept**	*set*
8	**huit**	*weet*
9	**neuf**	*nuhf*
10	**dix**	*deess*
11	**onze**	*oñz*
12	**douze**	*dooz*
13	**treize**	*trez*
14	**quatorze**	*ka-torz*
15	**quinze**	*kañz*
16	**seize**	*sez*
17	**dix-sept**	*dees-set*
18	**dix-huit**	*dees-weet*
19	**dix-neuf**	*dees-nuhf*
20	**vingt**	*vañ*
21	**vingt et un**	*vañt-ay-uñ*
22	**vingt-deux**	*vañ-duh*
30	**trente**	*troñt*
40	**quarante**	*ka-roñt*
50	**cinquante**	*sañ-koñt*
60	**soixante**	*swa-soñt*
70	**soixante-dix**	*swa-soñt-deess*
80	**quatre-vingts**	*katr-vañ*
90	**quatre-vingt-dix**	*katr-vañ-deess*
100	**cent**	*soñ*
110	**cent dix**	*soñ deess*
200	**deux cents**	*duh soñ*
1,000	**mille**	*meel*
1,000,000	**un million**	*uñ meel-yoñ*

1st	**premier**	*pruhm-yay*
2nd	**deuxième**	*duhz-yem*
3rd	**troisième**	*trwaz-yem*
4th	**quatrième**	*katr-yem*
5th	**cinquième**	*sañk-yem*
6th	**sixième**	*seez-yem*
7th	**septième**	*set-yem*
8th	**huitième**	*weet-yem*
9th	**neuvième**	*nuhv-yem*
10th	**dixième**	*deez-yem*

DAYS & MONTHS

JANVIER	JANUARY	**LUNDI**	MONDAY
FÉVRIER	FEBRUARY	**MARDI**	TUESDAY
MARS	MARCH	**MERCREDI**	WEDNESDAY
AVRIL	APRIL	**JEUDI**	THURSDAY
MAI	MAY	**VENDREDI**	FRIDAY
JUIN	JUNE	**SAMEDI**	SATURDAY
JUILLET	JULY	**DIMANCHE**	SUNDAY
AOÛT	AUGUST		
SEPTEMBRE	SEPTEMBER		
OCTOBRE	OCTOBER		
NOVEMBRE	NOVEMBER		
DÉCEMBRE	DECEMBER		

what's the date?
quelle est la date d'aujourd'hui?
kel ay la dat doh-zhoor-dwee

which day?
quel jour?
kel zhoor

which month?
quel mois?
kel mwa

March 5th
le 5 mars
luh sañk marss

July 6th
le six juillet
luh seess joo-yay

on Saturday
samedi
sam-dee

on Saturdays
le samedi
luh sam-dee

every Saturday
tous les samedis
too lay sam-dee

this Saturday
samedi qui vient
sam-dee kee vyañ

next Saturday
samedi prochain
sam-dee pro-shañ

last Saturday
samedi dernier
sam-dee dern-yay

please can you confirm the date?
vous pouvez me confirmer la date, s'il vous plaît?
voo poo-vay muh koñ-feer-may la dat seel voo play

TIME

Note that throughout Europe the 24-hour clock is used much more widely than in the UK.

what time is it, please?
quelle heure est-il, s'il vous plaît
kel uhr ayt-eel seel voo play

it's 1 o'clock
il est une heure
eel ay oon uhr

it's 3 o'clock
il est trois heures
eel ay trwaz uhr

it's half past 8
il est huit heures et demi
eel ay weet uhr ay duh-mee

in an hour
dans une heure
doñz oon uhr

half an hour
une demi-heure
oon duh-mee uhr

until 8 o'clock
jusqu'à huit heures
joos-ka weet uhr

it is half past 10
il est dix heures et demi
eel ay deez uhr ay duh-mee

at 10 am
à dix heures
a deez uhr

at 2200
à vingt-deux heures
a vañ-duhz uhr

at midday
à midi
a mee-dee

at midnight
à minuit
a meen-wee

soon
bientôt
byañ-toh

later
plus tard
ploo tar

---

du matin	**du soir**
doo ma-tañ	*doo swar*
am	pm

FOOD

ORDERING DRINKS

In cafés you are not charged immediately when you order a drink, so don't forget to pay before you leave.

a black coffee
un café noir
uñ ka-fay nwar

a white coffee
un café crème
uñ ka-fay krem

a tea
un thé
uñ tay

with milk
au lait
oh lay

with lemon
au citron
oh see-troñ

a bottle of mineral water
une bouteille d'eau minérale
oon boo-tay doh mee-ne-ral

sparkling
gazeuse
gaz-uhz

still
plate
plat

a beer
une bière
oon byehr

a shandy
un panaché
uñ pa-na-shay

a half pint
un demi
uñ duh-mee

what beers do you have?
qu'est-ce que vous avez comme bières?
kess kuh vooz a-vay kom byehr

the wine list, please
la carte des vins, s'il vous plaît
la kart day vañ seel voo play

a bottle of house wine
un pichet de vin
uñ pee-shay duh vañ

a glass of white/red wine
un verre de vin blanc/rouge
uñ vehr duh vañ bloñ/roozh

a bottle of red wine
une bouteille de vin rouge
oon boo-tay duh vañ roozh

a bottle of white wine
une bouteille de vin blanc
oon boo-tay duh vañ bloñ

would you like a drink?
voulez-vous boire quelque chose?
voo-lay voo bwar kel-kuh shoz

what will you have?
qu'est-ce que vous prenez?
kess kuh voo pruh-nay

ORDERING FOOD

can you recommend a good restaurant?
pouvez-vous nous recommander un bon restaurant?
poo-vay voo noo ruh-ko-moñ-day uñ boñ res-toh-roñ

I'd like to book a table
je voudrais réserver une table
zhuh voo-dray re-ser-vay oon tabl

for ... people
pour ... personnes
poor ... pehr-son

for tonight
pour ce soir
poor suh swar

at 8 pm
à huit heures
a weet uhr

the menu, please
le menu, s'il vous plaît
luh muh-noo seel voo play

is there a dish of the day?
est-ce qu'il y a un plat du jour?
ess keel ee a uñ pla doo zhoor

have you a set-price menu?
avez-vous un menu à prix fixe?
av-ay voo uñ muh-noo a pree feeks

I'll have this
je vais prendre ça
zhuh vay proñdr sa

what do you recommend?
qu'est-ce que vous me conseillez?
kess kuh voo muh koñ-say-ay

I don't eat meat
je ne mange pas de viande
zhuh nuh moñzh pa duh vyoñd

do you have any vegetarian dishes?
avez-vous des plats végétariens?
av-ay voo day pla ve-zhe-tar-yañ

excuse me!
excusez-moi!
eks-koo-say mwa

some bread please
du pain s'il vous plaît
doo pañ seel voo play

some water please
de l'eau s'il vous plaît
duh loh seel voo play

the bill, please
l'addition, s'il vous plaît
la-dees-yoñ seel voo play

bon appétit!
bon ap-e-tee
enjoy your meal!

61

FRENCH FOOD

French food is synonymous with excellence and travelling in France offers a wonderful opportunity to sample it. Over the centuries, great chefs, such as Escoffier, have created what is called **haute cuisine** (literally 'high-class cooking'), with elaborate sauces and beautiful presentation. The sauces are one of the essential elements that give French cuisine its character and style. Butter, wine, cream and sometimes truffles are among their main ingredients.

Nouvelle cuisine (literally 'new cookery', a style of preparing and presenting food, often raw with light sauces and unusual combinations of flavours and garnishes) and **cuisine minceur** (literally 'slimness cookery', a style which limits the use of starch, sugar, butter and cream) are developments that have taken place in recent years. Typically, dishes have a lower fat content, and portions are smaller but very attractively served. Each region has its own distinctive cuisine. The further inland you go the more likely you are to find genuine regional dishes. Whatever the style, French standards ensure that the food is enjoyable and of good quality.

THE MAIN CHARACTERISTICS OF THE REGIONS

WESTERN FRANCE

BRITTANY (Rennes)

In Brittany the food is simpler than in the rest of France. The region is known mainly for its superb seafood. Clams, lobster, scallops and oysters are to be found in delicious dishes, such as **coquilles Saint Jacques** (scallops **au gratin** baked in their shell), **homard à l'armoricaine** (a dish of lobster, onions, tomatoes and wine) and **cotriade**, a fish stew. The quality of the meat, mainly lamb, chicken and pork, is excellent, and the Bretons prepare marvellous pork pâtés (**pâtés de campagne**) and other pork products (**charcuterie**).

They love pancakes (**crêpes** and **galettes**) of various consistencies, from the very thin and delicate to a thicker savoury version made with buckwheat. Homely cakes are also a speciality, especially the **quatre-quarts** (so called because it is made with equal parts of butter, flour, sugar and eggs). The cheeses are generally mild in flavour. Good examples are **Port-Salut**, **Crémet Nantais** and **Campénéac**.

FRENCH FOOD

NORMANDY (Rouen)

This is dairy land and the cooking is rich with butter, cream, cider and **calvados** (apple brandy) used in many of the sauces. Its coastal position means that Normandy has its share of varied seafood. Try **sole normande** (sole with shrimps, cooked in cream and cider) and **moules marinière** (mussels with white wine, shallots and parsley). Some famous meat dishes are the **canard rouennais** (roast duck from Rouen, stuffed and covered with red wine sauce), **tripes à la mode de Caen** (tripe Caen style, stewed with trotters, carrots, onions, cider and Calvados), **poulet vallée d'Auge** (chicken cooked with cider, Calvados, apples and cream). **Andouilles** and **andouillettes** are smoked pork sausages and are especially good in Normandy.

Butter and cheeses are excellent, crowned by **Camembert**. **Pont l'Évêque**, **Excelsior**, **Cœur de Bray** and **La Bouille** are some of the many other Normandy cheeses. The region also excels in cakes and all manner of desserts, such as the **tarte normande** (apple tart), **mirlitons** (small almond tarts), and liqueur-filled chocolates.

The LOIRE VALLEY (Nantes)

Generally speaking, food here belongs to the national repertoire, although there are also a few local dishes, like pork-stuffed cabbage (**poitevin farci**) and **bardatte** (cabbage stuffed with hare or rabbit). Good **charcuterie**, **pâté** and **terrines** are very popular. **Rillettes** (baked minced meat) are excellent, made with pork, goose, rabbit or duck. There is excellent seafood and freshwater fish. **Bouilleture d'anguilles** is a dish made with eels, prunes and red wine. Don't miss **friture de la Loire** (tiny fried fish). There are also many kinds of mushrooms, often served raw in salads. Try also **truffiat**, a tasty potato cake.

The local dessert is **gâteau de Pithiviers**, a tart made with ground almonds. The region has very good pasture land which means the cheeses are of high quality. **Caillebotte**, **Crémet**, **Pithiviers au foin** and **Olivet bleu** are rich and on the mild side, while **Olivet cendré** tends to be strong. Among the goat's cheeses, the most famous is fresh **Chabichou**, but there are various other splendid ones, like **Valençay**, **Gien**, **Ste Maure** and **Couhé-Vérac**.

FRENCH FOOD

NORTHEASTERN FRANCE

The NORTH and CHAMPAGNE (Reims)

The North (Picardy, Artois and Flandres) and Champagne do not offer a distinctive regional cuisine, as their food is very similar to that of the surrounding areas. Flandres is the dominant influence, with such dishes as **carbonnade** (beef braised in beer) or **veau flamande** (veal cooked with dried apricots and prunes). Try **bouffis** or **craquelots** (smoked herrings) and **hareng saur** (again herring, salted and smoked). Pork products (**charcuterie**) are good and **terrines** are very popular, especially those made with game from the Ardennes. Some of the best cheeses are the strong **Maroilles**, the spicy **Puant de Lille**, **Caprice des Dieux** (mild), **Chaource** (mild) and **Langres**, with a strong smell, like many of the cheeses from these regions. Desserts and cakes are good, with many tarts made with fruit, **crêpes** (pancakes) and sweet **brioches** (sweet buns).

ALSACE (Strasbourg) and LORRAINE (Metz)

Alsace and Lorraine are very closely associated with the food from Germany. Pickled cabbage in the form of many sauerkraut (**choucroute**) variations is the main characteristic of regional dishes. **Choucroute garnie** (garnished sauerkraut) is the best known of these, and made with pork, sausages and potatoes. There are very good savoury flans, such as **flammekueche**, with cheese, onions, bacon and cream, and of course the famous **quiche lorraine** (with bacon and a rich egg custard). The **tourte à la lorraine** is yet another flan, with veal, pork and plenty of cream. **Baeckaoffa** is a mixture of beef, lamb and pork stewed in wine, and **coq au Riesling** is a chicken dish with cream, Riesling wine and mushrooms.

For dessert, there are many fruit tarts and an excellent variety of dried fruits. The cheeses such as **Munster** (the most well-known) and **Saint-Rémy** are generally strong, both in taste and smell. **Lorraine**, also called **Gérardmer**, is milder.

ÎLE de FRANCE and PARIS

Île de France and Paris are at the very heart of classic French **haute cuisine**, with its tempting **charcuterie**, smooth soups, rich sauces and sumptuous

FRENCH FOOD

cakes, using liberal amounts of butter and cream. Paris is the home of those sauces long associated with France as a whole, such as **hollandaise** (sauce made of butter, egg yolks and lemon, served warm) and **béchamel** (a white sauce made with flour, butter and milk), but it is also the place for the best **nouvelle cuisine**. The comparatively small area of the capital dominates France in matters of innovation and taste. While visiting Paris, if you want to concentrate on real French food, look around Les Halles and the Latin Quarter.

The famous rich **Brie**, king of cheeses, comes from the Île but is only one among various excellent cheeses, like the mild **Boursault**, the creamy **Explorateur** or the fresh **Fontainebleau**.

CENTRAL FRANCE AND THE ALPS

BURGUNDY (Dijon)

Bourgogne (Burgundy) is blessed with very fertile land and is, of course, a great wine region. The food here is robust and traditional in the best sense, with pork the favourite meat and therefore splendid **charcuterie**. A great speciality is **jambon** (cured ham) often served in local variations like **jambon persillé** (ham and parsley in aspic) and **jambon à la crème** (ham in wine, vinegar, cream and juniper berries). **Saucisse de Morteau** is a large smoked sausage typical of the region. Beef, chicken and game are also very good. Try **lièvre à la Piron** (a succulent dish of roasted hare with grapes), **bœuf bourguignon** (beef stewed in red wine) and **coq au vin** (chicken in red wine). Mushrooms and shallots or onions enrich the sauces of these and other dishes. Dijon mustard is also used in sauces. Offal is liberally used in hearty dishes, like **fressure** (pork offal in a stew made with red wine and herbs). Another local speciality are the snails (**escargots**) served with a sauce made of butter, parsley and garlic. The rivers provide freshwater fish, which is cooked simply and served with wine and cream sauces: **matelote**, a fish stew made with red wine, is a good example.

Desserts are not very numerous but try apple tart (**tartouillat**), **pognon** (a flat cake) and Dijon's **pain d'épices** (a kind of gingerbread). Cheeses include the strong **Pierre-Qui-Vire**, **Soumaintrain** fresh or cured, **Cîteaux** and **Époisses**. Goat's cheeses are also good. Try **Chevreton de Mâcon**, **Charollais** and **Claquebitou**.

FRENCH FOOD

MASSIF CENTRAL (Gorges du Tarn)

The Massif Central is a large rural area where you will find simple and hearty dishes based mainly on potatoes, cheese, cabbage and pork, such as **truffade** (mashed potato baked with cheese), **tourte à la viande** (a meat pie usually made with veal and pork), and **omelette brayaude** (a substantial omelette with cheese, ham and potatoes). Anything **à la limousine** will include chestnuts and red cabbage, to complement meat and game dishes. Wild mushrooms are also a feature here. Pork products (**charcuterie**) are excellent – try **picoussel** (a kind of pâté) and **pompe aux grattons** (pork flan). Vegetables are good and used in homely soups, such as **mourtaïrol** (beef, chicken, ham and vegetables), **cousinat** (chestnuts and cream) and **soupe aux choux** (cabbage and other vegetables with pork).

An abundance of fruit also means some rich desserts, including **clafoutis** (cherry pudding) and **gargouillau** (pear tart). There are many excellent cheeses, like **St. Nectaire**, **Fourme de Salers**, **Guéret**, and **Murol**, all quite mild, fresh **Tomme d'Aligot**, **Fourme de Laguiole** (strong) and **Bleu d'Auvergne** (a blue cheese). Goat's varieties include **Chevrotin du bourbonnais** and **Cabécou d'Entraygues**.

The RHÔNE VALLEY (Lyon)

The food is very good in this region, quite sophisticated in some places and plainer but still delicious in dishes like **pommes lyonnaise** (potatoes fried with onions). Pork, including offal, is liberally used and the **charcuterie** is excellent. **Cervelas aux truffes et pistaches** is a famous speciality consisting of **brioches** filled with sausages, truffles and pistachio nuts. **Rosette** and **sabodet** are two different kinds of pork sausage. Try **gratinée lyonnaise**, a clear soup with eggs, flavoured with port wine and served with toasted bread and cheese, **civet de lièvre** (a dish of hare cooked in wine, mushrooms and onions) and **poulet céléstine**, chicken cooked in wine, with mushrooms, tomatoes and cream. Freshwater fish is also used and **quenelles de brochet** are a speciality (pike mousse in cream sauce). For those who appreciate them, snails (**escargots**) and frogs' legs (**cuisses de grenouilles**) are of excellent quality here.

FRENCH FOOD

Desserts include **cocons**, almond sweets with liqueur, and **tendresses**, consisting of nougat with rum. Among the excellent cheeses, fresh **Cervelle de Claqueret** is definitely different, made with wine, herbs and vinegar. **Bleu de Bresse** is a good blue cheese, **Mont'Or** and **Rigotte de Condrieu** are mild. Goat's cheeses are all good (look for **petit Bressan**).

The ALPS and JURA

The Alps and Jura form a narrow, mountainous strip of land along the Swiss border. Food tends to be comforting and plain, with much use of pork. The **charcuterie** is varied and of the highest quality, and sometimes served in recipes including wine, such as **diots au vin blanc** (pork sausages in white wine). Freshwater fish appears in good basic dishes like **pauchouse** (a stew with wine) and in more elegant ones such as **quenelles de brochet** (pike mousse) and **sauce Nantua**, a sauce with freshwater crayfish, cream and truffles. Another local speciality is **brési**, smoked beef. But the real gastronomic seal of the area is the combination of potatoes and cheese, bacon or ham and cheese, or even cheese by itself, as in **fondue** (melted with wine). Try **gratin dauphinois** (sliced potatoes and cheese baked in milk). Cheese is sometimes added to vegetable soups, as in **soupe savoyarde**. Frogs' legs are also on the menu.

Nice desserts are **mont-blanc** (a chestnut and cream delight) and **gâteau grenoblois** (a walnut cake). There are many different cheeses. Some are blue, like **Bleu de Septmoncel**, **Bleu de Sassenage**, **Bleu de Sainte Foy** and others. Milder ones include **Cancoillotte**, **Morbier** and **Beaumont**. The main Swiss-type cheeses are **Gruyère de Comté** and **Emmenthal**. A few good goat's cheeses are **Tomme**, **Chevrotin** and **Persillé**.

SOUTHWESTERN FRANCE

POITOU, AQUITAINE (Bordeaux) and PÉRIGORD, QUERCY and the TOULOUSE region

As these regions include Bordeaux and Cognac, wine and spirits are of paramount importance and used in most dishes. Anything **à la bordelaise** includes red wine. **Verjus** (verjuice), the juice of unripe grapes, is also added to some sauces. Try **anguilles au verjus**, eels marinated in verjuice and grilled afterwards. Eels are actually greatly appreciated here,

FRENCH FOOD

as is lamprey. **Truffes** and **cèpes** (truffles and cep mushrooms) appear frequently on the menu. Along the coast seafood is excellent. Try **chaudrée rochelaise**, different kinds of fish stewed in wine. Oysters and mussels are obligatory items on the menu as well. The region grows the famous **charentais** melons and splendid vegetables. Périgord and Quercy comprise the famous Dordogne valley. Away from the sea, food concentrates more on earthy flavours, with the truffle as its most prized product. Despite its price, the truffle finds its way into many dishes and, together with **pâté de foie gras** (goose liver pâté), constitutes the hallmark of Périgourdine cuisine. Goose fat is preferred to any other and the bird itself, apart from its liver, is eaten mainly as a **confit** (cooked and preserved in its own fat), the carcass and giblets being used for homely soups. Sometimes one can find **oie farci aux pruneaux** (goose stuffed with the famous Agen prunes). **Cou d'oie farci** is goose neck stuffed with foie gras and truffles, served on its own or used to enrich other dishes. Plump chickens are made into rich dishes, like **tourtière** (a tart with salsify) or **cuisses de coquelets farcies** (chicken legs stuffed with meats and mushrooms and cooked in wine). There are many excellent omelettes, such as **omelette périgourdine aux cèpes** (cep omelette), and freshwater fish from the various local rivers is of very high quality. Try **truites grillées** (grilled trout). Beans appear in many dishes, like the local **cassoulet** (haricot bean stew with meats).

Sweets are varied as well, including various **beignets** (fritters), **tarte aux pommes** (apple tart) and **merveilles** (fritters flavoured with brandy). There aren't many varieties of cheese in these regions, but **Roquefort** – the best French blue, made with ewe's milk – is produced here and so is **Cabécou de Livernon**, a small cheese made with goat's milk.

The PYRÉNÉES (Bayonne)

Food throughout the region tends to be well-seasoned and spicy, showing a strong Spanish influence, with many warming stews, like **daube à la Béarnaise** (beef in wine) and **estouffat** (different kinds of meat, vegetables and wine or even Armagnac), and soups such as **braou bouffat** (cabbage and rice) or **garbure** (beans, meats and vegetables). In the north of the region goose is one of the favourite meats and made into **confit** (potted meat). Its liver is turned into **foie gras** but it can also be cooked with wine and grapes (**foie aux raisins**). There is very good ham in the region, especially from Bayonne, and many kinds of pork sausages, some similar to Spanish **chorizo**. Near Catalonia try dishes like **mouton à la catalane** (mutton and ham stewed in wine with a great deal of garlic) and **perdreau à la catalane** (partridge cooked in orange juice and peppers). In Roussillon olive oil and all the usual Mediterranean vegetables are used in strongly flavoured savoury dishes. There is game, as well as sea and freshwater fish, transformed into a variety of specialities, such as **salmis de palombes** (pigeon with wine) and **bouillinade** (a soupy fish stew with onions, peppers and garlic).

The region offers some good sweets, for example **pastis landais** (prune pastries), **cruchades** (a kind of pancake) and the delicious **gâteau Basquaise** (a plum cake). There are a few good ewe's cheeses made mainly for local consumption – try the strongly flavoured **Bethmale**.

THE SOUTH OF FRANCE

PROVENCE (Marseille)

Provençal gastronomy is as varied as its contrasting geographical conditions. Some areas are somewhat barren, sustaining only wild herbs, pine groves and grazing animals. The olive tree grows freely here, providing the olive oil and olives so much in use in the region. But the valleys along the Rhône are richly green and fertile. Garlic is the great ubiquitous element in Provence. **Aïoli** (garlic mayonnaise), which accompanies many dishes, and **aïgo bouïdo** (a bread soup with garlic) are two examples. Around Nice anchovies are part of various delicacies, like **salade niçoise**, which includes boiled eggs, lettuce, tomatoes, olives and peppers. The other great port is Marseilles, where the main speciality is **bouillabaisse**, a mixed fish soup highly seasoned and flavoured with saffron. There are various other local fish soups, such as **soupe de poisson** and **bourride**. Salt cod is used in **brandade de morue**, a garlicky mixture of pureed salt cod with milk or cream and olive oil, and **stocaficada**, a stew. Italian influence reveals itself in pasta dishes, a pizza-like flan called **pissaladière**, and the inclusion of basil in many recipes, for example **soupe au pistou**, a vegetable soup mixed with a sauce (**pistou**) made of garlic, basil, olive oil and cheese, similar to Italian pesto. Peppers, aubergines and tomatoes are cooked with olive oil in dishes like **ratatouille**.

FRENCH FOOD

With so many savoury delicacies, sweets are not prominent here, but try **calissons**, made with ground almonds. Cheeses are mainly goat's and ewe's, and are delicious. Look for **Tomme de Camargue**, **Picodon de Valréas** and **Banon**.

LANGUEDOC (Nîmes)

In Languedoc regional dishes make liberal use of aubergines, tomatoes and olive oil. The Mediterranean coast provides good mussels, oysters, sardines and other fish. Salt cod is also used in **brandade**. Two delicacies are **civet de langouste** (crayfish cooked in wine and garlic) and **langouste à la sétoise**, crayfish with cognac, tomatoes and the omnipresent garlic. The region is famous for its meat dishes, mostly made from pork in all its forms. **Cassoulet**, the well-known bean stew which includes pork and Toulouse sausages, is a typical Languedoc dish. Tripe and offal in general are much used, especially inland (try **gras double**, tripe and onions cooked in wine) as well as goose or duck and goose fat. Chestnuts, all kinds of pulses, wild mushrooms and truffles are also local specialities. Try **escargots à la languedocienne** (snails with anchovies, walnuts and cured pork) and **cargolade** (snails stewed in wine).

There are splendid sweets all over Languedoc. The best are perhaps **marrons glacés** (glacé chestnuts).

CORSICA (Ajaccio)

The culinary traditions from the South of France are carried on in Corsica (Corse), although here there is a strong influence from Italy as well. Corsican cuisine is highly seasoned and hearty. There is wild boar on the island and a very good pâté is made with it. Seafood is popular, and there are some very good dishes made with squid. Try also sea urchins, a local delicacy. Freshwater fish (mainly trout) are abundant too. **Charcuterie** is varied and excellent. Olive trees guarantee olive oil and olives for the kitchens and chestnuts are a speciality here. Cheeses for local consumption are made with goat's and ewe's milk.

SOME SPECIALITIES FROM OTHER FRENCH-SPEAKING EUROPEAN COUNTRIES

BELGIUM

Belgian cuisine is not what immediately springs to mind when talking about food, but the truth is that the country offers a surprising variety of local specialities. There are more than 350 brands of beer in Belgium. Most of the produce comes from the Brabant region where the cuisine owes much to the use of beer in sauces and stews. It's even used in soups (**consommé au fumet de malt**). Endives, Brussels sprouts and mussels are Belgian specialities. Seafood is plentiful and herrings a local obsession, prepared in many tasty dishes, like **harengs grillés en fillets** (grilled herring fillets) and **boestring** (smoked herring). Sole and plaice are also appreciated. Other specialities are **croquettes bruxelloises**, with mussels, and **omelette bruxelloise**, made with smoked herrings. But the most popular dish of all is mussels and chips. **Carbonnade à la bière** (meat braised in beer) can be made either with pork or beef. Chicken, tripe dishes, sausages and all kinds of **charcuterie** are also popular.

For dessert, try **tarte au corin** (a tart made either with dried fruits or with cheese and cream), **cougnous** (a cake served at Christmas), **tarte au maton** (made with buttermilk and also a celebration sweet), and the traditional **gaufres** (waffles). In Brussels there are various typical sweets, like beer fritters, **spéculos** (a spicy cake) and **cakes de Bruxelles**, containing dried fruit. Chocolate truffles, pralines and toffees are also a speciality. Belgium has many fine cheeses, each region having different varieties.

LUXEMBOURG

Absorbing influences from all the neighbouring countries, Luxembourg makes them its own. The cuisine is unpretentious and mostly peasant in origin, but also reflects some refinement. Soups are often served as starters – try, for example, nettle soup (**brennesselszopp**), very delicate in flavour, or potato soup (**gromperenzopp**) with leeks and milk. Freshwater fish (trout, pike, crayfish) is used in dishes like pike in green sauce (**hietcht mat kraïderzooss**) and **friture de la Moselle** (small fried fish from the Moselle river). Mussels (**moulen**) are popular in dishes like **moules marinière** and **moules à la luxembourgeoise**. There are also

FRENCH FOOD

many pork specialities, such as cured ham and black pudding (**trèipen**) and suckling pig in aspic (**fierkelsjhelli**). Dumplings are popular, either made with potato (**gromperekniddelen**) or buckwheat (**stäerzelen**).

Desserts include **quetscheflued**, a plum tart, **kèiskuch**, cheese cake, and **äppelkuch**, apple cake. Festive cakes are served on St Nicholas Day on the 6th December (**boxemännercher**, ginger bread men) and during the carnival season (**verwurrelt gedanken**, fried cakes).

SWITZERLAND

The food of the French-speaking part of Switzerland is influenced by France, and even by Italy. Meals are hearty and tend to start with a soup, like onion with cheese or pea purée with pork, for example. Cheese is one of the main ingredients in countless dishes, especially starters and light meals. Many include bread, as in cheese toast **à la vaudoise** and **croûtes au fromage**. Swiss **fondue** (cheese melted in wine in which pieces of bread are dipped) is of course popular all over the country, with local variations. The lakes and rivers are full of fish (pike, perch and trout). Try **fillets de perche à la meunière** (perch cooked in butter and served with butter and wine sauce), **perche au gratin** (baked in béchamel sauce) and trout mousse from Jura, a rather grand dish accompanied by a cream sauce. Veal is used in a hot meat pie, and Valais hot-pot consists of bacon with vegetables, cooked slowly in stock and wine, and served with cooked dried pears. **Roesti** is a very Swiss dish (fried, grated potatoes, formed into a round flat cake browned on both sides). Try **Valais roesti**, which includes onion. **Croûte aux champignons** is mushrooms in a rich sauce, served on toast. Near the Italian border, **pitz** (a kind of pizza with tomatoes) is a popular dish.

For dessert, apricot flan is a favourite in Valais, as well as **sii**, a pudding made with mashed bread, wine, fruit and cream. **Gaufrettes** are cones made of a rich dough and filled with cream. In season, strawberries in wine and in jelly are served in Valais.

FRENCH FOOD

EATING OUT

Meals taken in restaurants in France are generally leisurely affairs – which is just as well, as food of this quality shouldn't be rushed. The main meal used to be lunch (**déjeuner**), served between 12.30 and 2.30 pm. Nowadays, lunch may be smaller with dinner (**dîner**) as the main meal, served between the hours of 7 and 10 pm. Breakfast (**petit déjeuner**) is served between 7.30 and 9.30 am. This is a light meal, consisting of bread (**pain**), **croissants**, or **brioches**, and a large cup of black coffee or coffee with hot milk (**café au lait**). You will also be given **beurre** (butter) and **confiture** (jam).

Brasseries, **snack-bars** and **cafés** may serve a big breakfast with eggs and ham, and they also serve snacks during the day. If you just want a drink or coffee without food, look for a bar. You can also buy food and drink to take away or for picnics at a **pâtisserie** (cake shop), **boulangerie** (baker's) or **charcuterie** (cold meats). These shops generally close at lunch time but open early (about 7 am) and close between 7 and 8 pm. However, there are places which sell take-away snacks any time, in which case you will find a sign announcing this (**sandwichs** or **casse-croûte**).

In villages you cannot always find a snack at odd hours of the day, so if you are travelling in rural areas it might be a good idea to buy something at a food store to take with you. In towns and cities fast food (hamburgers and pizzas) is available at the usual chains. **Traiteurs** (delicatessens and caterers) are also a good source of take-away food. They often have ready-to-eat dishes of a high standard for you to take home. Note that at restaurants you are always given bread (generally without butter) to eat with your meal. And in some places, **vin ordinaire** might be offered without charge. If there is a **spécialité de la maison** (speciality of the house), it is always worth considering. Some establishments have a set menu (**menu à prix fixe** or **menu touristique**) which is almost always very good value. Vegetables and salads are generally served separately from the fish or meat dishes.

Good ideas for snacks or light meals include toasted sandwiches (**croque-monsieur**, with ham and cheese, or **croque-madame**, with an added egg), **crêpes** (pancake), **omelette** and **frites** (chips).

FRENCH FOOD

EATING PLACES AND TYPES OF FOOD SERVED

Auberge similar to a restaurant, generally outside town and also offering accommodation.

Bar serves drinks and snacks, and sometimes breakfasts as well.

Bar-brasserie also serves drinks and snacks.

Buffet (at airports and train stations) self-service, average quality and value.

Cabaret (or **boîte de nuit**) drinks and food served, with dancing.

Café serves soft and alcoholic drinks, coffee, etc. It may also have snacks.

Crêperie specialises in **crêpes** (pancakes) and is generally cheap, good for a light meal.

Libre service self-service eateries at supermarkets. Ordinary cheap meals.

Restaurant for complete, protracted meals. The menu should be on view outside. A good choice is the **plat du jour** (dish of the day).

Restoroute road-side self-service restaurant.

Rôtisserie restaurant serving barbecue food.

Routier (or **relais routier**) road-side restaurants favoured by truck drivers. Ordinary fare but good quality and value.

Salon de thé (tea room) these are on the expensive side, serving tea and excellent cakes, generally from an attached **pâtisserie**. Tea is served weak, and perhaps with lemon (**au citron**). If you do not like weak tea or do not want it without milk, you must order specifically what you want. **Tisanes** (herbal teas) are always available.

FRENCH FOOD

READING THE MENU

Before ordering your meal you should find out whether there are additional charges, like taxes and service. In some places, these charges may have already been included in the price (**service compris**).

la carte general menu, in detail.

menu menu (normally a set menu).

menu du jour menu of the day.

menu dégustation this is a menu sometimes found in top restaurants, giving small servings of various dishes (tastings) so customers can sample them all without becoming too full up.

menu gastronomique a gastronomic menu, carefully chosen with special dishes. It may be expensive.

table d'hôte set menu.

Menu headings vary from place to place and may include:

entrées/hors d'œuvres *starters/appetizers/first course*

pâtés et terrines *pâtés and terrines*

potages *soups*

assiette anglaise *platter of cold meats*

salades *salads*

légumes *vegetables*

pâtes *pasta (spaghetti, etc)*

plat de résistance *main course*

spécialité de la maison *speciality of the house*

spécialités de la région *regional dishes*

viandes *meats*

gibier et volaille *game and poultry*

poissons et coquillages *fish and shellfish*

œufs *eggs*

desserts *desserts (tarts, puddings, ice cream, sorbet)*

fromages *cheeses*

fruits *fruit*

DRINKS

DRINKS

The simplest of drinks is water and there are excellent bottled waters in France. Coffee (black and strong) is a national passion, but tea is less popular, served weak and without milk, unless you specifically ask for it. Herbal teas (**tisanes**), on the other hand, are popular, and there are many to choose from. French beer (**bière**) is generally of the lager type. However, near the German and Belgian borders it has more body. Cider (**cidre**) is a favourite drink in Brittany and even more so in Normandy.

WINES and LIQUEURS

France is a nation of wine drinkers and great wines – the best in the world. Each region naturally promotes its own wines, but the best restaurants will also offer a wider range, embracing all the best produce, albeit at a price. If what you want is a reasonably good wine with your meals, then **vin ordinaire** or **vin de table** (house wine) served in a **carafe** or even by the glass will almost always be very satisfactory and reasonably priced. Opting for local wine also has the advantage of solving what goes best with the local food. The production of wine is carefully monitored by the **Institut National des Appelations d'Origine**, which assigns each wine to a particular category. These categories are, by order of merit, **AOC (Appelation Contrôlée)**, **VDQS (Vin Délimité de Qualité Supérieur)**, **Vins de Pays** (good quality regional wines) and **Vins de Table** (ordinary table wine, varying in quality).

The main wines from the Loire are white and dry, using Sauvignon Blanc grapes. They are made in Sancerre, Pouilly, Ménétou-Salon, Quincy and Reuilly. In the area of Touraine, the main grape is the white Chenin Blanc, used in Vouvray and Montlouis. On the other hand, the reds of Chinon, Bourgueil, Saint-Nicolas-de-Bourgueil and Saumur-Champigny are made from Cabernet Franc grapes. However, Saumur is better known for its sparkling wines and Anjou-Saumur for rosé. Try the dry white Muscadet also from the Loire region .

The grapes used to make the famous sparkling wine of the Champagne region are Chardonnay, Pinot Noir and Pinot Meunier. Reims, Épernay and Châlons-sur-Marne are the towns around which champagne is made. What makes this wine different is the so-called **méthode champenoise**, involving a second fermentation in the bottle and other procedures which guarantee the sparkle and the ageing.

In Alsace the wines are very German in type, with very good Riesling, Gewurztraminer, Pinot Blanc, Tokay-Pinot Gris, Muscat and other excellent whites, ranging from very dry to sweet. Alsace also produces a few good light reds.

Burgundy is one of the major wine-producing areas of the world, with excellent reds and whites. The main grape varieties used are the Chardonnay for whites and Pinot Noir for the reds, the main areas to remember being Chablis, Côte de Nuits, Côte de Beaune, Côte Chalonnaise, the Mâconnais and of course Beaujolais. This is a region of Burgundy, producing mainly reds from Gamay grapes, and a few whites from the Chardonnay. Beaujolais Nouveau is made to be drunk while young. However other wines from the region can have ageing potential, such as Brouilly, Chénas, Chiroubles, Côte de Brouilly, Fleurite, Juliénas, Morgon, Moulin-à-Vent, Régnié and Saint-Amour.

The northern Rhône produces mainly red wine from the Syrah grape. It includes the wines of Hermitage, Côte Rôtie, Saint-Joseph, Crozes-Hermitage and Cornas. There is also some white wine and sparkling wine from Saint-Péray. The southern part of the region produces mainly reds from different varieties of grape in Châteauneuf-du-Pape, Gigondas, Tavel and Lirac. Côtes du Rhône, Côtes du Ventoux and Côtes du Vivarais must of course be mentioned. The region also has dessert wines, Muscat de Beaumes-de-Venise and Rasteau.

Bordeaux is perhaps the most celebrated French wine region. The best wines are from the Médoc, with Cabernet Sauvignon, Cabernet Franc, Merlot, Malbec and Petit Verdot grapes. But look out for wines made in Saint-Émilion and Pomerol, which are made mainly with Merlot grapes. South of the Médoc there are good reds and whites from the Graves area. However, for sweet whites nothing is better than the Sauterne and Barsac areas. Entre-Deux-Mers is famous for dry whites.

Liqueurs are another French speciality, and some are world famous, like **Chartreuse**. France is famous also for **cognacs**, with well-loved (and expensive) brands like Remy-Martin, Courvoisier, and Martel. **Armagnacs** have a richer colour but are similarly good, though perhaps less well-known.

DRINKS

Abricotine *liqueur brandy with apricot flavouring*
armagnac *fine grape brandy from the Landes area*
Badoit *mineral water, very slightly sparkling*
Bénédictine *herb liqueur on a brandy base*
bière *beer*
bière pression *draught beer*
bière blonde *lager*
bière brune *bitter*
café *coffee*
café au lait *coffee with hot milk*
café crème *white coffee*
café décaféiné *decaffeinated coffee*
café express *espresso coffee*
café glacé *iced coffee*
café irlandais *Irish coffee*
café noir *plain black coffee*
calvados *apple brandy made from cider (Normandy)*
cassis *blackcurrant liqueur*
Chartreuse *aromatic herb liqueur made by Carthusian monks*
chocolat *chocolate (hot and rich tasting)*
cidre *cider, sparkling (**bouché**) or still, quite strong*
cidre doux *sweet cider*
citron pressé *freshly squeezed lemon juice with water and sugar*
cognac *high quality white grape brandy*
Cointreau *orange-flavoured liqueur*
Contrexeville *mineral water (still)*
crème de menthe *peppermint-flavoured liqueur*
Curaçao *orange-flavoured liqueur*
diabolo menthe *mint cordial and lemonade*
eau de Seltz *soda water*
eau-de-vie *brandy (often made from plum, pear, etc)*
eau douce *fresh water*
eau minérale *mineral water*

DRINKS

eau minerale gazeuse *sparkling mineral water*
eau nature *plain water*
eau potable *drinking water*
Evian *mineral water (still)*
Grand Marnier *tawny-coloured, orange-flavoured liqueur*
Izarra vert *green-coloured herb liqueur*
jus de pomme *apple juice*
jus d'orange *orange juice*
kir *white wine and* **cassis** *aperitif*
kirsch *a kind of* **eau-de-vie** *made from cherries (Alsace)*
lait *milk*
Mirabelle *plum brandy from Alsace*
orangeade *orangeade*
pastis *name given to aniseed-flavoured aperitifs*
Pernod *aperitif with aniseed flavour (***pastis***)*
Perrier *mineral water (sparkling)*
St Raphael *aperitif (with quinine)*
thé *tea*
thé au citron *tea with lemon*
thé au lait *tea with milk*
thé sans sucre *tea without sugar*
tilleul *lime herbal tea*
tisane *herbal tea*
verveine *herbal tea made with verbena*
Vichy *mineral water (sparkling)*
vin *wine*
vin blanc *white wine*
vin de pays *regional wine*
vin de table *table wine*
vin rosé *rosé wine*
vin rouge *red wine*
Vittel *mineral water (still)*
Volvic *mineral water (still)*

MENU READER

...à l'/à la/au/aux *in the style of*
...à l'anglaise *poached or boiled*
...à l'armoricaine *with brandy, wine, tomatoes and onions*
...à la bonne femme *cooked in white wine with mushrooms*
...à la bordelaise *with a sauce made with red wine and vegetables*
...à la bourguignonne *in red wine, with onions, bacon and mushrooms*
...à la colbert *fried, with a coating of egg and breadcrumbs*
...à la dauphinoise *cooked in milk*
...à la flamande *served with potatoes, cabbage, carrots and pork*
...à la jardinière *with peas and carrots, or other fresh vegetables*
...à la lyonnaise *with onions*
...à la marinière *a sauce of white wine, onions and herbs (mussels or clams)*
...à la meunière *dusted in flour and sautéed in butter*
...à la mornay *with cheese sauce*
...à la niçoise *with garlic and tomatoes*
...à la paysanne *with potatoes and other vegetables*
...à la provençale *with tomatoes, peppers and garlic*
...à la vapeur *steamed*
...au gratin *browned on top, with breadcrumbs and grated cheese*
...aux herbes *with fresh herbs*
abats *offal; giblets*
abricot *apricot*
agneau *lamb*
aiglefin *haddock*
ail *garlic*
aïoli *garlic mayonnaise*
airelles *bilberries; cranberries*
amande *almond*
ananas *pineapple*
anchoïade *anchovies on toast, with garlic*
anchois *anchovies*
andouille *sausage made with chitterlings*
anguille *eel*
anis *aniseed*
arachide *peanut (uncooked)*
araignée de mer *spider crab*
artichaut *artichoke*
artichauts à la barigoule *artichokes in wine, with carrots, garlic, onions*

artichauts châtelaine *artichokes stuffed with mushrooms*
asperge *asparagus*
assiette anglaise *platter with some cold meats*
assiette de charcuterie *platter with assorted sausages*
assiette de crudités *selection of raw vegetables served with a dip*
aubergine *aubergine*
aubergines farcies *stuffed aubergines*
aurin *grey mullet*
avocat *avocado*
babas au rhum *yeast cake soaked in syrup with rum*
baccala frittu *dried salt cod fried Corsica style*
baguette *stick of French bread*
banane *banana*
bar *sea-bass*
barbue *brill*
basilic *basil*
batavia *Webb lettuce*
bavarois *moulded cream and custard pudding, usually served with fruit*
bécasse *woodcock*
béchamel *white sauce made with milk*
beignets *fritters*
betterave *beetroot*
beurre *butter*
bifteck *steak*
bifteck à point *medium rare steak*
bifteck au poivre *steak with peppercorns*
bifteck bien cuit *well done steak*
bifteck bleu *very rare steak*
bifteck saignant *rare steak*
bifteck tartare *raw steak minced and mixed with tartare sauce*
bis *wholemeal (of bread or flour)*
biscotin *biscuit*
bisque *seafood soup*
bisque de homard *lobster soup*
blanquette de veau *veal in white sauce*
blanquette de volaille *chicken in a rich white sauce with mushrooms and herbs*
blé *wheat*
bœuf *beef*

MENU READER

bœuf bourguignon *beef in burgundy, onions and mushrooms*
bœuf en daube *a rich beef stew with wine, vegetables and herbs*
bombe *moulded ice cream dessert*
bonbons *sweets*
bonite *bonito, small tuna fish*
boudin blanc *white pudding, made from white meat, cream and eggs*
boudin noir *black pudding*
bouillabaisse *seafood soup flavoured with saffron*
bouilli *boiled*
brandade de morue *dried salt cod puréed with cream and olive oil*
brème *bream*
brioche *sweet bun*
brioche aux fruits *sweet bun soaked in liqueur and covered with fruit*
brochet *pike*
brochette d'agneau *lamb kebab*
brocoli *broccoli*
brugnon *nectarine*
cabillaud *fresh cod*
cacahuète *peanut (salted or roasted)*
caille *quail*
caille sur canapé *quail served on toast*
caillettes *rolled liver stuffed with spinach*
calmar *(or* **calamar***) squid*
canard *duck*
canard à l'orange *roast duck with orange sauce*
canard sauvage *wild duck*
cannelle *cinnamon*
câpres *capers*
carbonnade de bœuf *braised beef*
cari *curry*
carotte *carrot*
carottes vichy *carrots in butter*
carpe *carp*
carpe farcie *carp stuffed with mushrooms or* **foie gras**
carré persillé *roast lamb Normandy style (with parsley)*
carrelet *plaice*
cassis *blackcurrant; blackcurrant liqueur*
cassoulet *bean stew with different kinds of meat, according to region*
caviar blanc *mullet roe*

caviar niçois *a paste made with anchovies and olive oil*
cédrat *large citrus fruit, similar to a lemon*
céleri *celery*
céleri-rave *celery root*
céleri rémoulade *shredded celery with mustard mayonnaise*
cèpes *boletus mushrooms; wild mushrooms*
cèpes marinés *marinated mushrooms*
cerfeuil *chervil*
cerise *cherry*
cervelas *smoked pork sausages*
cervelle *brains*
champignon *mushroom*
champignons à la grècque *mushrooms cooked in wine and olive oil*
champignons de Paris *button mushroom*
champignons périgourdine *mushrooms with truffles and **foie gras***
chanterelle *chanterelle (wild golden-coloured mushroom)*
chantilly *whipped cream*
châtaigne *chestnut*
châteaubriand aux pommes *tender steak with fried potatoes*
chaud(e) *hot*
chausson *a pasty filled with meat or seafood*
chèvre *goat*
chevreuil *venison*
chicorée *chicory (for coffee); endive*
chocolat *chocolate*
chou *cabbage*
chou-fleur *cauliflower*
choux brocolis *broccoli*
choux de Bruxelles *Brussels sprouts*
citron *lemon*
citron vert *lime*
citrouille *pumpkin*
cives (or ciboulettes) *chives*
civet de langouste *lobster in wine sauce*
civet de lièvre *hare stewed in wine, onions and mushrooms*
clafoutis *cherry pudding*
clou de girofle *clove*
cochon *pig*
coco *coconut*

MENU READER

cœur *heart*
cœur d'artichauts *artichoke hearts*
cœurs de palmier *palm hearts*
coing *quince*
colin *hake*
compote de fruits *mixed stewed fruit*
concombre *cucumber*
condé *rich rice pudding with fruits*
confit d'oie *goose pâté*
confit de canard *potted duck*
confiture *jam*
confiture d'oranges *marmalade*
consommé *clear soup*
contre-filet *sirloin fillet (beef)*
coq *cockerel*
coq au vin *chicken cooked in red wine*
coquillages *shellfish*
coquilles à la provençale *scallops with garlic sauce*
coquilles Saint-Jacques *scallops cooked in the shell with a breadcrumb and cheese topping*
coquillettes *pasta shells*
cornichon *gherkin*
côte *rib; chop*
côtelette *cutlet*
côtes de veau *veal chops*
cotriade *fish stew (Brittany)*
courge *marrow*
coussinet *cranberry*
crabe *crab*
crème *cream*
crème anglaise *egg custard*
crème au beurre *butter cream with egg yolks and sugar*
crème brûlée *rich custard with caramelised sugar on top*
crème chantilly *whipped cream with sugar*
crème d'argenteuil *white asparagus soup*
crème de cresson *watercress soup*
crème renversée (or **crème caramel**) *custard with a caramelised top*
crêpes fourrées *filled pancakes*
crêpes Suzette *pancakes with Cointreau or Grand Marnier sauce*

crépinette *type of sausage*
crevette *prawn*
crevette grise *shrimp*
crevette rouge *large prawn*
crevettes en terrine *potted prawns*
crudités *raw vegetables*
crustacés *shellfish*
cuisses de grenouille *frogs' legs*
culotte *rump steak*
datte *date*
dindon (or **dinde**) *turkey*
échalote *shallot*
échine *loin of pork*
écrevisse *freshwater crayfish*
églefin *haddock*
en brochette *cooked like a kebab (on a skewer)*
encornet *squid*
endive *chicory*
entrecôte *rib steak*
entremets *sweets (desserts)*
épaule *shoulder*
épice *spice*
épinards *spinach*
escalope *escalope*
escargots *snails (generally cooked with strong seasonings)*
escargots à la bourguignonne *snails with garlic butter*
espadon *swordfish*
estragon *tarragon*
esturgeon *sturgeon*
faisan *pheasant*
farci(e) *stuffed*
faux-filet *sirloin*
faverolles *haricot beans*
fenouil *fennel*
feuilleté aux fraises *strawberry tart*
figue *fig*
filet de bœuf en croûte *steak in pastry*
filet de bœuf *tenderloin*
filet *fillet*

MENU READER

filet mignon *small fillet steak*
fine de claire *type of oyster*
fines herbes *mixed herbs*
flageolet *type of small green haricot bean*
flétan *halibut*
flocons d'avoine *rolled oats*
florentine *with spinach, usually served with mornay sauce*
foie *liver*
foie gras *goose liver pâté*
fond d'artichaut *artichoke heart*
fondue (au fromage) *melted cheeses into which chunks of bread are dipped*
fondue bourguignonne *small chunks of meat dipped into boiling oil*
fougasse *type of bread*
fraise *strawberry*
fraises des bois *wild strawberries*
framboise *raspberry*
fricassée de poulet *chicken fricassée*
frisée *curly endive*
frit(e) *fried*
friture *fried food, usually small fish*
froid(e) *cold*
fromage *cheese*
fromage blanc *soft white cheese*
fromage frais *creamy fresh cheese*
fruit *fruit*
fruits de mer *shellfish, seafood*
fumé(e) *smoked*
galantine *meat in aspic*
galette *savoury pancake*
gambas *large prawns*
garbure *thick vegetable and meat soup*
garni(e) *garnished*
gâteau *cake, gateau*
gâteau Saint-Honoré *choux pastry cake filled with custard*
gaufres *waffles (often filled with cream)*
gelée *jelly, aspic*
genièvre *juniper berry*
génoise *sponge cake*

gibier *game*
gigot *leg of lamb*
glace *ice cream*
goyave *guava*
graines de soja *soya beans*
gratin, au *topped with cheese and breadcrumb and grilled*
grenouilles meunière *frogs' legs cooked in butter*
grillé(e) *grilled*
gros mollet *lump fish*
groseille *redcurrant*
groseille à maquereau *gooseberry*
hareng *herring*
haricots *beans*
haricots blancs *haricot beans*
haricots rouges *red kidney beans*
haricots verts *green beans, French beans*
herbes (fines herbes) *herbs*
homard *lobster*
homard thermidor *lobster served in cream sauce, topped with parmesan*
hors d'œuvres variés *varied appetizers*
huile *oil*
huile d'arachide *groundnut oil*
huile de tournesol *sunflower oil*
huître *oyster*
jambon *ham*
jambon cru *cured (raw) ham*
jambon cuit *cooked ham*
jambon de Paris *boiled ham*
julienne *vegetables cut into fine strips*
jus *juice; gravy*
lait *milk*
lait demi-écrémé *semi-skimmed milk*
lait écrémé *skimmed milk*
lait entier *full-cream milk*
laitue *lettuce*
lamproie à la bordelaise *lamprey in red wine*
langouste *crayfish (saltwater)*
langouste froide *crayfish served cold with mayonnaise and salad*
langoustines *scampi (large)*

MENU READER

langue *tongue*
langue de chat *type of narrow biscuit*
lapin *rabbit*
lapin chasseur *rabbit cooked in wine*
lard *fat; streaky bacon*
lard fumé *smoked bacon*
lard maigre *lean bacon*
lardon *strip of fat; diced bacon*
laurier *bayleaf*
légumes *vegetables*
lentilles *lentils*
levure *yeast*
lièvre *hare*
lotte *monkfish*
loup de mer *sea-bass*
macédoine (de fruits) *fruit salad*
macédoine de légumes *mixed cooked vegetables*
madeleine *small sponge cake*
maïs; maïs doux *maize; sweetcorn*
mange-tout *sugar peas*
maquereau *mackerel*
marcassin *young wild boar*
marjolaine *marjoram*
marron *chestnut*
marrons glacés *candied chestnuts*
matelote à la normande *sea-fish stew with cider, Calvados and cream*
médaillon *thin, round slice of meat*
menthe *mint; mint tea*
meringues à la chantilly *meringues filled with whipped cream*
merlan *whiting*
merluche *hake*
merou *grouper*
mignonnette *small fillet of lamb*
mille-feuille *thin layers of pastry filled with cream and jam*
mirabelle *small yellow plum; plum brandy*
mont-blanc *pudding made with chestnuts and cream*
morue *dried salt cod*
moules *mussels*
moules poulette *mussels in wine, cream and mushroom sauce*

MENU READER

mousse au chocolat *chocolate mousse*
moutarde *mustard*
mouton *mutton; sheep or lamb*
mûre *blackberry*
muscade *nutmeg*
myrtille *bilberry*
navet *turnip*
noisette *hazelnut*
noisettes d'agneau *small round pieces of lamb, fillet, rib or topside*
noix *walnut; general term for a nut*
nouilles *noodles*
œuf *egg*
œufs à la causalade *fried eggs with bacon*
œufs à la coque *soft-boiled eggs*
œufs à la tourangelle *eggs served with red wine sauce*
œufs Bénédicte *poached eggs on toast, with ham and hollandaise sauce*
œufs brouillés *scrambled eggs*
œufs durs *hard-boiled eggs*
œufs en cocotte *eggs baked in individual containers*
œufs frits *fried eggs*
oie *goose*
oignon *onion*
olive *olive*
omelette *omelette*
orange *orange*
orge *barley*
os *bone*
oseille *sorrel*
pain *bread; loaf of bread*
pain au chocolat *croissant with chocolate filling*
pain bis *brown bread*
pain complet *wholemeal bread*
pain de mie *white sliced loaf*
pain de seigle *rye bread*
pain grillé *toast*
palombe *wood pigeon*
palourde *clam*
pamplemousse *grapefruit*
panais *parsnip*

MENU READER

pané(e) *with breadcrumbs*
parfait *rich ice cream with fruits and cream*
Paris Brest *ring-shaped cake filled with hazelnut-flavoured cream*
parmentier *with potatoes*
pastis *aniseed-based aperitif*
patate douce *sweet potato*
pâté *pâté*
pâté de foie de volailles *chicken liver pâté*
pâté en croûte *pâté encased in pastry*
pâtes *pasta*
paupiettes *meat slices stuffed and rolled*
pêche *peach*
perche *perch (fish)*
perche du Menon *perch cooked in champagne*
perdreau (perdrix) *partridge*
persil *parsley*
persillé(e) *with parsley*
petit pain *roll*
petit-beurre *butter biscuit*
petits pois *small peas*
pièce de bœuf *special cut of beef*
pigeon *pigeon*
pignons *pine nuts*
pilon *drumstick (chicken)*
piment doux *sweet pepper*
piment fort *chilli*
piment *red pepper*
pintade/pintadeau *guinea fowl*
pipérade *tomato, pepper and onion omelette*
pissaladière *flan with anchovies, tomatoes and olives*
pistache *pistachio*
pistou *garlic, basil and olive oil sauce – similar to pesto*
plie *plaice*
poché(e) *poached*
poire *pear*
poireau *leek*
poires belle Hélène *poached pears with vanilla ice cream and hot chocolate sauce*
pois *peas*

MENU READER

pois cassés split peas
pois-chiches chickpeas
poisson fish
poitrine breast (lamb or veal)
poivre pepper
poivron sweet pepper
pomme apple
pomme de terre potato
pommes de terre à l'anglaise boiled potatoes
pommes de terre à la vapeur steamed potatoes
pommes de terre allumettes match-stick chips
pommes de terre dauphine small potatoes in pastry, fried
pommes de terre duchesse potato mashed then baked in the oven
pommes de terre frites fried potatoes
pommes de terre mousseline potatoes mashed with cream
pommes de terre rissolées small potatoes deep-fried
porc pork
pot au feu beef and vegetable stew
potiron type of pumpkin
poulet chicken
poulet basquaise chicken stew with wine, tomatoes and peppers
poulet demi-deuil chicken breasts in a wine sauce
poulpe à la niçoise octopus in tomato sauce
pousses de soja bean sprouts
praire clam
praliné hazelnut flavoured
prune plum; plum brandy
pruneau prune; damson (Switz.)
purée de pommes de terre mashed potatoes
quenelles de brochet pike mousse in cream sauce
quetsch type of plum
queue de bœuf oxtail
radis radish
ragoût stew; casserole
raie skate
raifort horseradish
raisin grape
raisin sec sultana; raisin
raisin de mars redcurrant (Switzerland only)

MENU READER

ramier *wood pigeon*
râpé(e) *grated*
rascasse *scorpion fish*
ratatouille *tomatoes, aubergines, courgettes and garlic cooked in olive oil*
rave *turnip*
reine-claude *greengage*
rillettes de canard *potted minced duck*
rillettes de porc *potted minced pork*
ris de veau *calf sweetbread*
riz *rice*
rognon *kidney*
rognons sautés sauce madère *sautéed kidneys served in Madeira sauce*
romaine *cos lettuce*
romarin *rosemary*
romsteak *rump steak*
rond de gigot *large slice of leg of lamb*
rosbif *roast beef*
rôti *roast*
rouget *red mullet*
rouille *spicy hot sauce for fish*
roulade *meat or fish, stuffed and rolled*
roulé *sweet or savoury roll*
rutabaga *swede*
sabayon *dessert made with egg yolks, sugar and Marsala wine*
sablé *shortbread*
safran *saffron*
Saint-Hubert *game consommé flavoured with wine*
salade aveyronnaise *cheese salad (made with Roquefort)*
salade de fruits *fruit salad*
salade de saison *mixed salad and/or greens in season*
salade *lettuce; salad*
salade lyonnaise *vegetable salad (cooked), dressed with anchovies and capers*
salade niçoise *salad with mixed vegetables (raw and cooked), anchovies, olives and lettuce*
salade russe *mixed cooked vegetables in mayonnaise*
salsifis *salsify*
sanglier *wild boar*
sarriette *savory (herb)*

sauce *sauce*
sauce bordelaise *red wine, bone marrow and shallots*
sauce chasseur *wine sauce with shallots and mushrooms.*
sauce hollandaise *butter, egg yolks and lemon juice, served warm*
sauce Mornay *cream and cheese sauce*
sauce Périgueux *with truffles*
saucisse/saucisson *sausage*
saumon *salmon*
saumon fumé *smoked salmon*
saumon poché *poached salmon*
sauté(e) *sautéed*
sauté d'agneau *lamb stew*
scarole *endive; escarole*
sec *dry or dried*
seiche *cuttlefish*
sel *salt*
selle d'agneau *saddle of lamb*
semoule *semolina*
sole *sole*
sole Albert *sole in cream sauce with mustard*
sole cardinal *sole cooked in wine, served with lobster sauce*
sole Saint Germain *grilled sole with butter and tarragon sauce*
sole-limande *lemon sole*
soufflé au fromage *cheese soufflé*
soufflé au Grand Marnier *soufflé flavoured with Grand Marnier liqueur*
soufflé au jambon *ham soufflé*
soupe *soup*
soupe à l'oignon *onion soup topped with bread and cheese, toasted on top*
soupe à la bière *beer soup*
soupe au pistou *vegetable soup with garlic and basil*
soupe de poisson *fish soup*
steak *beef steak*
sucre *sugar*
suprême de volaille *breast of chicken in cream sauce*
sur le grill *grilled*
tarte aux fraises *strawberry tart*
tarte aux pommes *apple tart*
tarte tatin *upside down tart with caramelized apples or pears*

MENU READER

terrine *terrine; pâté*
terrine de campagne *pork and liver terrine*
terrine de porc et gibier *pork and game terrine*
tétras *grouse*
thon *tuna fish*
tilleul *lime tea*
timbale d'écrevisses *crayfish in a cream, wine and brandy sauce*
timbale de fruits *pastry base covered with fruits*
tomate *tomato*
tomates à la provençale *grilled tomatoes, with garlic*
tomates farcies *stuffed tomatoes*
tomme *type of cheese*
tournedos *thick fillet steak*
tripes *tripe*
truffade *potato pie with garlic and cheese*
truffe *truffle*
truite *trout*
truite aux amandes *trout covered with almonds*
vacherin *large meringue filled with cream, ice cream and fruit*
veau *calf, veal*
veau sauté Marengo *veal cooked in white wine, with onions, tomato and garlic*
venaison *venison*
verjus *juice of unripe grapes*
vermicelle *vermicelli*
viande *meat*
viande séchée *thin slices of cured beef*
vichyssoise *leek and potato soup, served cold*
vinaigrette *French dressing of oil and vinegar*
vinaigre *vinegar*
volaille *poultry*
yaourt *yoghurt*
zewelwai *onion flan*

DICTIONARY
english-french
french-english

A

a(n) un (m)/une (f) see GRAMMAR
abbey l'abbaye (f)
able: to be able to pouvoir see GRAMMAR
abortion l'avortement (m)
abortion pill la pilule abortive
about (approx) vers ; environ
  about 100 francs environ cent francs
  about 10 o'clock vers dix heures
above au-dessus (de)
  above the bed au-dessus du lit
  above the farm au-dessus de la ferme
abroad à l'étranger
abscess l'abcès (m)
accelerator l'accélérateur (m)
to accept accepter
accident l'accident (m)
accommodation le logement
account le compte
to ache faire mal
  it aches ça fait mal
acid l'acide (m)
adaptor (electrical) l'adaptateur (m)
adder (snake) la vipère
address l'adresse (f)
  what is the address? quelle est l'adresse?
address book le carnet d'adresse
admission charge l'entrée (f)
adult m/f l'adulte
  for adults pour adultes
advance: in advance à l'avance
advertisement (in newspaper) l'annonce (f)
  (on TV) la publicité
to advise conseiller
aeroplane l'avion (m)
aerosol l'aérosol (m)
afraid: to be afraid of something avoir peur de quelque chose
after après

afternoon l'après-midi (m)
  in the afternoon l'après-midi (m)
  this afternoon cet après-midi
  tomorrow afternoon demain après-midi
aftershave l'après-rasage (m)
again encore
against contre
age l'âge (m)
agency l'agence (f)
ago: a week ago il y a une semaine
to agree être d'accord
agreement l'accord (m)
AIDS le SIDA
airbag (in car) l'airbag (m)
air-conditioning la climatisation
  is there air-conditioning? c'est climatisé?
air freshener le désodorisant
airline la ligne aérienne
air mail: by airmail par avion
air mattress le matelas pneumatique
airplane l'avion (m)
airport l'aéroport (m)
airport bus la navette pour l'aéroport
air ticket le billet d'avion
aisle le couloir
alarm l'alarme (f)
alarm clock le réveil
alcohol-free sans alcool
alcoholic alcoolique
  is it alcoholic? c'est alcoolisé?
all tout(e)/tous/toutes
allergic allergique
  I'm allergic to... je suis allergique à...
allergy l'allergie (f)
to allow permettre
  it's not allowed c'est interdit ; c'est défendu
all right (agreed) d'accord
  are you all right? ça va?

almond l'amande (f)

almost presque

alone tout(e) seul(e)

Alps les Alpes

already déjà

also aussi

altar l'autel (m)

always toujours

am see (to be) GRAMMAR

amber (traffic light) orange

ambulance l'ambulance (f)

America l'Amérique (f)

American américain(e)

anaesthetic l'anesthésique (m)
a local anaesthetic une anesthésie locale
a general anaesthetic une anesthésie générale

anchor l'ancre (f)

anchovies les anchois

and et

angel l'ange (m)

angina l'angine de poitrine (f)

angry fâché(e)

animal l'animal (m)

aniseed l'anis (m)

ankle la cheville

anniversary l'anniversaire (m)

annual annuel(-elle)

another un(e) autre
another beer une autre bière

answer la réponse

to answer répondre à

answerphone le répondeur

antacid le comprimé contre les brûlures d'estomac

antibiotic l'antibiotique (m)

antifreeze l'antigel (m)

antihistamine l'antihistaminique (m)

antiques les antiquités

antique shop le magasin d'antiquités

antiseptic l'antiseptique (m)

any de (du/de la/des) see GRAMMAR
have you any apples? vous avez des pommes?

apartment l'appartement (m)

apéritif l'apéritif (m)

appendicitis l'appendicite (f)

apple la pomme

apple juice le jus de pomme

application form le formulaire

appointment le rendez-vous
I have an appointment (at 10) j'ai rendez-vous (à 10 heures)

apricot l'abricot (m)

April avril (m)

apron le tablier

architect m/f l'architecte

architecture l'architecture (f)

are see (to be) GRAMMAR

arm le bras

armbands (for swimming) les bracelets gonflables

armchair le fauteuil

aromatherapy l'aromathérapie (f)

to arrange arranger

to arrest arrêter

arrival l'arrivée (f)

to arrive arriver

art l'art (m)

art gallery le musée

arthritis l'arthrite (f)

artichoke l'artichaut (m)

artificial artificiel

artist l'artiste (m/f)

ashtray le cendrier

to ask demander

asparagus les asperges

aspirin l'aspirine (f)
soluble aspirin l'aspirine effervescente

asthma l'asthme (m)
I have asthma je suis asthmatique

at à
at my/your/his home chez moi/vous/lui

at 8 o'clock à huit heures
at once tout de suite
at night la nuit
attack *(mugging)* l'agression *(f)*
(medical) la crise
to attack agresser
attic le grenier
attractive attrayant(e)
aubergine l'aubergine *(f)*
auction la vente aux enchères
audience le public
August août *(m)*
aunt la tante
au pair la jeune fille au pair
Australia l'Australie *(f)*
Australian australien(ne)
author l'écrivain ; l'auteur *(m)*
automatic automatique
automatic *(car)* la voiture à boîte
automatique
auto-teller le distributeur
automatique (de billets)

autumn l'automne *(m)*
available disponible
avalanche l'avalanche *(f)*
avenue l'avenue *(f)*
avocado l'avocat *(m)*
to avoid éviter
awful affreux(-euse)
axle *(car)* l'essieu *(m)*

B

baby le bébé
baby food les petits pots
baby milk *(formula)* le lait maternisé
baby's bottle le biberon
baby seat *(in car)* le siège pour
bébés
babysitter le/la babysitter
baby wipes les lingettes
back *(of body)* le dos
backpack le sac à dos
bacon le bacon, le lard

bad *(food, weather)* mauvais(e)

bag le sac
(suitcase) la valise
baggage les bagages
baggage allowance le poids (de
bagages) autorisé
baggage reclaim la livraison des
bagages
bait *(for fishing)* l'appât *(m)*
baker's la boulangerie
balcony le balcon
bald *(person)* chauve
(tyre) lisse
ball *(large: football, etc)* le ballon
(small: golf, tennis, etc) la balle
ballet le ballet
balloon le ballon
banana la banane
band *(music)* le groupe
bandage le pansement
bank *(money)* la banque
(river) la rive ; le bord
bank account le compte en
banque
banknote le billet de banque
bar le bar
barbecue le barbecue
to have a barbecue faire un
barbecue
barber's le coiffeur
barcode le code barres
to bark aboyer
barn la grange
barrel *(wine, beer)* le tonneau
basement le sous-sol
basil le basilic
basket le panier
basketball le basket-ball
bat *(baseball, cricket)* la batte
(animal) la chauve-souris
bath le bain
to have a bath prendre un bain
bathing cap le bonnet de bain
bathroom la salle de bains
with bathroom avec salle de
bains

battery *(for car)* la batterie
  (for radio, camera, etc) la pile
bay *(along coast)* la baie
bay leaf la feuille de laurier
to be être *see* **GRAMMAR**
beach la plage
  private beach la plage privée
  sandy beach la plage de sable
beach hut la cabine
bean le haricot
  broad bean la fève
  french/green bean le haricot vert
  kidney bean le haricot rouge
  soya bean la graine de soya
bear *(animal)* l'ours(e)
beard la barbe
beautiful beau (belle)
beauty salon le salon de beauté
because parce que
to become devenir
bed le lit
  double bed le grand lit ; le lit
  de deux personnes
  single bed le lit d'une personne
  sofa bed le canapé-lit
  twin beds les lits jumeaux
bed clothes les couvertures
bedroom la chambre à coucher
  my bedroom ma chambre
bee l'abeille (f)
beech le hêtre
beef le bœuf
beer la bière
beetroot la betterave
before avant
to begin commencer
behind derrière
beige beige
Belgian belge
Belgium la Belgique
to believe croire
bell *(church, school)* la cloche
  (doorbell) la sonnette
below sous

belt la ceinture
  money belt la ceinture
  porte-monnaie
  seatbelt la ceinture de sécurité
bend *(in road)* le virage
berth *(train, ship, etc)* la couchette
beside *(next to)* à côté de
  beside the bank à côté de la
  banque
best le/la mieux
to bet on faire un pari sur
better meilleur(e)
  better than meilleur que
between entre
bib *(baby's)* le bavoir
bicycle la bicyclette ; le vélo
bicycle repair kit la trousse de
  réparation (pour vélo)
bidet le bidet
big grand(e)
bike *(pushbike)* le vélo
  (motorbike) la moto
  mountain bike le vélo tout
  terrain (le VTT)
bike lock l'antivol (m)
bikini le bikini
bilberry la myrtille
bill *(restaurant)* l'addition (f)
  (hotel) la note
  (for work done) la facture
bin *(dustbin)* la poubelle
bin liner le sac poubelle
binoculars les jumelles
bird l'oiseau (m)
biro le stylo
birth certificate l'acte de
  naissance (m)
birthday l'anniversaire (m)
  happy birthday! bon anniversaire!
  my birthday is on... mon
  anniversaire c'est...
birthday card la carte
  d'anniversaire
birthday present le cadeau
  d'anniversaire
biscuits les biscuits

b

bishop l'évêque (m)
bit: *a bit (of)* un peu (de)
bite (animal) la morsure
  (insect) la piqûre
bitten (by animal) mordu(e)
  (by insect) piqué(e)
bitter amer(-ère)
black noir(e)
blackberry la mûre
blackcurrant le cassis
black ice le verglas
blanket la couverture
bleach l'eau de Javel (f)
to bleed saigner
blender (for food) le mixeur
blind (person) aveugle
blind (for window) le store
blister l'ampoule (f)
block of flats l'immeuble
blocked bouché(e)
  the sink is blocked l'évier est
  bouché

b

blond (person) blond(e)
blood le sang
blood group le groupe sanguin
blood pressure la tension
  (artérielle)
blood test l'analyse de sang (f)
blouse le chemisier
blow-dry le brushing
blue bleu(e)
  dark blue bleu foncé
  light blue bleu clair
boar (wild) le sanglier
boarding card la carte d'embarquement
boarding house la pension (de
  famille)
boat le bateau
  (rowing) la barque
boat trip l'excursion en bateau (f)

b

body le corps
  (clothing) le body
to boil faire bouillir
boiled bouilli(e)

bomb la bombe
bone l'os (m)
  (fish) l'arête (f)
bonfire le feu
book le livre
to book (reserve) réserver
booking la réservation
booking office le bureau de
  location
bookshop la librairie
boots les bottes
  (short) les bottillons
border (of country) la frontière
boring ennuyeux
to borrow emprunter
boss le chef
both les deux
bottle la bouteille
  a bottle of wine une bouteille
  de vin
  a bottle of water une bouteille
  d'eau
  a half-bottle une demi-bouteille
bottle opener l'ouvre-bouteilles (m)
bottom (of pool, etc) le fond
  (buttocks) le derrière
bowl (for soup, etc) le bol
  washing up bowl la cuvette
bow tie le nœud papillon
box la boîte
box office le bureau de location
boxer shorts le boxer-short
boy le garçon
boyfriend le copain
bra le soutien-gorge
bracelet le bracelet
brake(s) le(s) frein(s)
to brake freiner
brake fluid le liquide de freins
branch (of tree) la branche
  (of company, etc) la succursale
brand (make) la marque
brandy le cognac
brass le cuivre

brave courageux(-euse)
bread le pain
  (French stick) la baguette
  (thin French stick) la ficelle
  sliced bread le pain en tranches
breadcrumbs les miettes
bread roll le petit pain
to break casser
breakable fragile
breakdown *(car)* la panne
  (nervous) la dépression
breakdown van la dépanneuse
breakfast le petit déjeuner
breast *(of chicken)* le blanc
to breathe respirer
brick la brique
bride la mariée
bridegroom le marié
bridge le pont
  (game) le bridge
briefcase la serviette
Brillo® pad le tampon Jex®
to bring apporter
Britain la Grande Bretagne
British britannique
broccoli le brocoli
brochure la brochure ; le dépliant
broken cassé(e)
  my leg is broken je me suis
  cassé la jambe
broken down *(car, etc)* en panne
bronze le bronze
brooch la broche
broom *(brush)* le balai
brother le frère
brother-in-law le beau-frère
brown marron
bruise le bleu
brush la brosse
Brussels sprouts les choux de
  Bruxelles
bubble bath le bain moussant
bucket le seau
buffet car *(train)* la voiture-buffet
to build construire

building *(flats, etc)* l'immeuble *(m)*
bulb *(light)* l'ampoule *(f)*
bumbag la banane
bumper *(on car)* le pare-chocs
bunch *(of flowers)* le bouquet
  (of grapes) la grappe
bungee jumping le saut à
  l'élastique
bureau de change le bureau de
  change
burger l'hamburger *(m)*
burglar le/la cambrioleur(-euse)
to burn brûler
bus le bus
bus pass la carte de bus
bus station la gare routière
bus stop l'arrêt de bus *(m)*
bus ticket le ticket de bus
business les affaires
  on business pour affaires
business card la carte de visite
business class la classe affaires
businessman/woman l'homme/la
  femme d'affaires
business trip le voyage d'affaires
busy occupé(e)
but mais
butcher's la boucherie
butter le beurre
butterfly le papillon
button le bouton
to buy acheter
by *(via)* par
  (beside) à côté de
  by bus en bus
  by car en voiture
  by ship en bateau
bypass *(road)* la rocade

C

cab *(taxi)* le taxi
cabaret le cabaret
cabbage le chou
cabin *(on boat)* la cabine

C

cablecar le téléphérique ; la benne
cable TV la télévision par câble
café le café
  internet café le cybercafé
cafetiere la cafetière
cake (large) le gâteau
  (small) la pâtisserie
cake shop la pâtisserie
calculator la calculatrice
calendar le calendrier
calf (young cow) le veau
call (telephone) l'appel (m)
to call (speak, phone) appeler
calm la calme
camcorder le caméscope
camera l'appareil photo (m)
camera case l'étui (m)
camera shop le magasin de photo
to camp camper
camping gas le butane
camping stove le réchaud de camping
campsite le camping
can la boîte
can (to be able to) pouvoir see GRAMMAR
can opener l'ouvre-boîtes (m)
Canada le Canada
Canadian canadien(ne)
canal le canal
to cancel annuler
cancellation l'annulation (f)
cancer le cancer
candle la bougie
canoe le canoë
to go canoeing faire du canoë-kayak
cap (hat) la casquette
  (diaphragm) le diaphragme
capital (city) la capitale
cappuccino le cappucino
car la voiture
car alarm l'alarme de voiture (f)
car ferry le ferry

car hire la location de voitures
car insurance l'assurance automobile (f)
car keys les clés de voiture
car phone le téléphone de voiture
car port l'auvent (pour voiture) (m)
car radio l'autoradio (m)
car seat (for children) le siège pour enfant
car wash le lave-auto
carafe le pichet
caravan la caravane
carburettor le carburateur
card la carte
  birthday card la carte d'anniversaire
  business card la carte de visite
  playing cards les cartes à jouer
cardboard le carton
cardigan le cardigan
careful: to be careful faire attention
  careful! attention!
carnation l'œillet (m)
carpet (rug) le tapis
  (fitted) la moquette
carriage (railway) la voiture
carrot la carotte
to carry porter
carving knife le couteau à découper
case (suitcase) la valise
cash l'argent liquide (m)
to cash (cheque) encaisser
cash desk la caisse
cash dispenser (ATM) le distributeur automatique (de billets)
cashier le/la caissier(-ière)
casino le casino
casserole dish la cocotte
cassette la cassette
cassette player le magnétophone
castle le château
casualty department les urgences

cat le chat
catalogue le catalogue
catch *(bus, train)* prendre
cathedral la cathédrale
Catholic catholique
cauliflower le chou-fleur
cave la grotte
CD le CD
CD player le lecteur de CD
ceiling le plafond
celery le céleri
cellar la cave
cemetery le cimetière
centimetre le centimètre
central central(e)
central heating le chauffage
central locking le verrouillage
central
centre le centre
century le siècle
   19th century le dix-neuvième
siècle
ceramic la céramique
certain *(sure)* certain(e)
certificate le certificat
chain la chaîne
chair la chaise
chairlift le télésiège
chalet le chalet
champagne le champagne
change *(small coins)* la monnaie
to change changer
   to change money changer de
l'argent
   to change clothes se changer
   to change bus changer d'autobus
   to change train changer
de train
changing room la cabine
d'essayage
Channel *(English)* La Manche
chapel la chapelle
charcoal le charbon de bois
cheap bon marché
cheaper moins cher

to check vérifier
to check in enregistrer
check-in (desk) *(at airport)*
l'enregistrement des bagages *(m)*
   (at hotel) la réception
cheek la joue
cheers! santé!
cheese le fromage
cheeseburger le hamburger au
fromage
chef le chef de cuisine
chemist's la pharmacie
cheque le chèque
cheque book le carnet de chèques
cheque card la carte d'identité
bancaire
cherry la cerise
chest *(body)* la poitrine
chest of drawers la commode
chestnut la châtaigne
chewing gum le chewing-gum
chicken le poulet
chickenpox la varicelle
chickpea le pois chiche
child l'enfant *(m)*
child safety seat *(car)* le siège
pour enfant
children les enfants
   for children pour enfants
chilli le piment rouge
chimney la cheminée
chin le menton
china la porcelaine
chips les frites
chives la ciboulette
chocolate le chocolat
   hot chocolate le chocolat chaud
   drinking-chocolate le chocolat
(en poudre)
chocolates les chocolats
choir la chorale
to choose choisir
chop *(meat)* la côtelette
chopping board la planche à
découper

christening le baptême
Christmas Noël *(m)*
  merry Christmas! joyeux Noël!
Christmas card la carte de Noël
Christmas Eve la veille de Noël
chrysanthemum le chrysanthème
church l'église *(f)*
cider le cidre
cigar le cigare
cigarette la cigarette
cigarette lighter le briquet
cigarette paper le papier à
  cigarette
cinema le cinéma
circle *(theatre)* le balcon
circuit breaker le disjoncteur
circus le cirque
city la ville
city centre le centre-ville
class la classe
  first-class de première classe
  second-class de seconde classe
clean propre
to clean nettoyer
cleanser *(for face)* le démaquillant
clear clair(e)
client le client/la cliente
cliff *(along coast)* la falaise
  (in mountains) l'escarpement
to climb *(mountain)* faire de la
  montagne
climbing boots les chaussures de
  montagne
Clingfilm® le Scellofrais®
clinic la clinique
cloakroom le vestiaire
clock l'horloge *(f)*
close by proche
to close fermer
closed *(shop, etc)* fermé(e)
cloth *(rag)* le chiffon
  (fabric) le tissu
clothes les vêtements
clothes line la corde à linge

clothes peg la pince à linge
clothes shop le magasin de
  confection
cloudy nuageux(-euse)
cloves *(spice)* le girofle
club le club
clutch *(in car)* l'embrayage *(m)*
coach *(bus)* le car ; l'autocar *(m)*
coach station la gare routière
coach trip l'excursion en car *(f)*
coal le charbon
coast la côte
coastguard le garde-côte
coat le manteau
coat hanger le cintre
Coca-Cola® le Coca®
cockroach le cafard
cocktail le cocktail
cocoa le cacao
coconut la noix de coco
coffee le café
  white coffee le café au lait
  black coffee le café noir
  cappuccino le cappuccino
  decaffeinated coffee le café
  décaféiné
coil *(IUD)* le stérilet
coin la pièce de monnaie
Coke® le Coca®
colander la passoire
cold froid
  I'm cold j'ai froid
  it's cold il fait froid
cold water l'eau froide *(f)*
cold *(illness)* le rhume
  I have a cold j'ai un rhume
cold sore le bouton de fièvre
collar le col
collar bone la clavicule
colleague le/la collègue
to collect *(someone)* aller chercher
colour la couleur
colour-blind daltonien(ne)
colour film *(for camera)* la pellicule
  couleur

comb le peigne
to come venir *see* **GRAMMAR**
  (to arrive) arriver
  to come back revenir
  to come in entrer
  come in! entrez!
comedy la comédie
comfortable confortable
company *(firm)* la compagnie ; la
  société
compartment le compartiment
compass la boussole
to complain faire un réclamation
complaint la plainte
compulsory obligatoire
computer l'ordinateur *(m)*
computer disk *(floppy)* la disquette
computer game le jeu
  électronique
computer program le programme
  informatique
computer software le logiciel
concert le concert
concert hall la salle de concert
concession la réduction
concussion la commotion
  (cérébrale)
conditioner l'après-shampooing *(m)*
condom le préservatif
conductor *(on bus)* le receveur
conference la conférence
to confirm confirmer
congratulations félicitations!
connection *(bus, train, etc)* la
  correspondance
constipated constipé(e)
consulate le consulat
to contact contacter
contact lenses les verres de
  contact
contact lens cleaner le produit
  pour nettoyer les verres de
  contact
to continue continuer
contraceptive le contraceptif

contract le contrat
to cook *(be cooking)* cuisiner
  to cook a meal préparer un
  repas
cooked cuisiné
cooker la cuisinière
cool frais (fraîche)
cool-box *(for picnic)* la glacière
copper le cuivre
copy *(duplicate)* la copie
to copy copier
coral le corail
coriander la coriandre
cork le bouchon
corkscrew le tire-bouchon
corner le coin
corridor le couloir
cortisone la cortisone
cost le coût
to cost coûter
  how much does it cost? ça
  coûte combien?
cot le lit d'enfant
cottage la maison de campagne
cotton le coton
cotton bud le coton-tige®
cotton wool le coton hydrophile
couchette la couchette
cough la toux
to cough tousser
cough mixture le sirop pour la
  toux
cough sweets les pastilles pour
  la toux
counter *(shop, bar, etc)* le comptoir
country *(not town)* la campagne
  (nation) le pays
countryside le paysage
couple *(two people)* le couple
courgette la courgette
courier service le service de
  messageries
course *(syllabus)* le cours
  (of meal) le plat
cousin le/la cousin(e)

cover charge (restaurant) le couvert
cow la vache
crab le crabe
crafts (gifts, etc) les objets artisanaux
craftsman/woman l'artisan(e)
cramp (pain) la crampe
cramps (period pain) les règles douloureuses
crash (car) l'accident (m) ; la collision
crash helmet le casque
cream (food, lotion) la crème
  soured cream la crème aigre
  whipped cream la crème fouettée
credit card la carte de crédit
crime le crime
crisps les chips
croissant le croissant
cross la croix
to cross (road, sea, etc) traverser
cross-country skiing le ski de fond
crossing (by sea) la traversée
crossroads le carrefour ; le croisement
crossword puzzle les mots croisés
crowd la foule
crowded bondé(e)
crown la couronne
cruise la croisière
crutches les béquilles
to cry (weep) pleurer
crystal le cristal
cucumber le concombre
cufflinks les boutons de manchette
cul-de-sac le cul-de-sac
cumin le cumin
cup la tasse
cupboard le placard
currant le raisin sec
currency la devise ; la monnaie
current (air, water, etc) le courant
cursor (computer) le curseur
curtain le rideau

cushion le coussin
custard la crème anglaise
custom (tradition) la tradition
customer le/la client(e)
customs la douane
  (duty) les droits de douane
customs declaration la déclaration de douane
to cut couper
cutlery les couverts
cycle le vélo ; la bicyclette
cycle track la piste cyclable
cycling le cyclisme
cyst le kyste
cystitis la cystite

D

daffodil la jonquille
daily (each day) tous les jours
daisy la pâquerette
damage les dégâts
damp humide
dance le bal
to dance danser
danger le danger
dangerous dangereux(-euse)
dark l'obscurité (f)
  after dark la nuit tombée
date la date
date of birth la date de naissance
daughter la fille
daughter-in-law la belle-fille ; la bru
dawn l'aube (f)
day le jour
  per day par jour
dead mort(e)
deaf sourd(e)
dear (expensive, in letter) cher (chère)
decaffeinated décaféiné(e)
  decaffeinated coffee le café décaféiné
December décembre

deckchair la chaise longue
to declare: *nothing to declare*
rien à déclarer
deep profond(e)
deep freeze le congélateur
to defrost décongeler
to de-ice *(windscreen)* dégivrer
delay le retard
how long is the delay? il y a
combien de retard?
delicatessen l'épicerie fine *(f)*
delicious délicieux(-euse)
dental floss le fil dentaire
dentist le/la dentiste
dentures le dentier
deodorant le déodorant
to depart partir
department store le grand
magasin
departure le départ
departure lounge la salle d'embarquement
deposit les arrhes
to describe décrire
description la description
desk *(furniture)* le bureau
dessert le dessert
details les détails
detergent le détergent
detour la déviation
to develop *(photos)* faire
développer
diabetes le diabète
diabetic diabétique
I'm diabetic je suis diabétique
to dial *(a number)* composer (un
numéro)
dialling code l'indicatif *(m)*
dialling tone la tonalité
diamond le diamant
diapers les couches pour bébé
diarrhoea la diarrhée
diary l'agenda *(m)*
dice le dé
dictionary le dictionnaire

to die mourir
diesel le gas-oil
diet le régime
I'm on a diet je suis au régime
different différent(e)
difficult difficile
dinghy le youyou
dining room la salle à manger
dinner *(evening meal)* le dîner
to have dinner dîner
direct *(train, etc)* direct(e)
directions les indications
directory *(telephone)* l'annuaire *(m)*
directory enquiries (le service
des) renseignements
dirty sale
disabled *(person)* handicapé(e)
to disappear disparaître
disaster la catastrophe
disco la discothèque
discount le rabais
to discover découvrir
disease la maladie
dish le plat
dishwasher le lave-vaisselle
disinfectant le désinfectant
disk *(computer)* le disque
floppy disk la disquette
hard disk le disque dur
to dislocate *(joint)* disloquer
disposable nappies les couches
jetables
distant lointain(e)
distilled water l'eau distillée *(f)*
district *(of town)* le quartier
to disturb déranger
to dive plonger
diversion la déviation
divorced divorcé(e)
I'm divorced je suis divorcé(e)
DIY shop le magasin de bricolage
dizzy pris(e) de vertige
to do faire *see* GRAMMAR
doctor le médecin
documents les papiers

d

dog le chien
dog lead la laisse
doll la poupée
dollar le dollar
domestic flight le vol intérieur
dominoes les dominos
donut le beignet
door la porte
doorbell la sonnette
double double
double bed le grand lit
double room la chambre pour
  deux personnes
doughnut le beignet
down: to go down descendre
downstairs en bas
dragonfly la libellule
drain *(house)* le tuyau d'écoule-
  ment
draught *(of air)* le courant d'air
  there's a draught il y a un
  courant d'air
draught lager la bière pression
drawer le tiroir
drawing le dessin
dress la robe
to dress s'habiller
dressing *(for food)* la vinaigrette
dressing-gown le peignoir
drill *(tool)* la perceuse électrique
drink la boisson
to drink boire
drinking chocolate le chocolat
  chaud
drinking water l'eau potable *(f)*
to drive conduire
driver *(of car)* le conducteur/la
  conductrice
driving licence le permis de
  conduire
drought la sécheresse
drug *(medicine)* le médicament
  (narcotics) la drogue
drunk ivre ; soûl(e)
dry sec (sèche)

to dry sécher
dry-cleaner's le pressing
duck le canard
dummy *(for baby)* la sucette ; la
  tétine
during pendant
dust la poussière
duster le chiffon
dustpan and brush la pelle et la
  balayette
duty-free hors taxe
duty-free shop la boutique hors
  taxe
duvet la couette
duvet cover la housse de couette
dye la teinture
dynamo la dynamo

E

each chacun/chacune
eagle l'aigle *(m)*
ear l'oreille *(f)*
  my ears mes oreilles
earlier plus tôt
early tôt
earn gagner
earphones le casque
earrings les boucles d'oreille
earth la terre
earthquake le tremblement de
  terre
east l'est *(m)*
Easter Pâques *(fpl)*
  happy Easter! joyeuses Pâques!
Easter egg l'œuf de Pâques
easy facile
to eat manger
ebony l'ébène *(f)*
eel l'anguille *(f)*
egg l'œuf *(m)*
  fried eggs les œufs sur le plat
  hard-boiled egg l'œuf dur
  scrambled eggs les œufs
  brouillés

soft-boiled egg l'œuf à la coque
egg white le blanc d'œuf
egg yolk le jaune d'œuf
either: *either one* l'un ou l'autre
elastic band l'élastique (m)
elastoplast® le sparadrap
elbow le coude
electric électrique
electric razor le rasoir électrique
electrician l'électricien (m)
electricity l'électricité (f)
electricity meter le compteur
 électrique
elevator l'ascenseur (f)
e-mail le courrier éléctronique ;
 le e-mail
 to e-mail sb envoyer un e-mail à
 qn
e-mail address l'addresse
 éléctronique
embassy l'ambassade (f)
emergency l'urgence (f)
emergency exit la sortie de
 secours
empty vide
end la fin
engaged (to be married) fiancé(e)
 (phone, toilet etc) occupé(e)
engine le moteur
engineer m/f l'ingénieur
England l'Angleterre (f)
English anglais(e)
 (language) l'anglais (m)
to enjoy aimer
 I enjoy swimming j'aime nager
 I enjoy dancing j'aime danser
enough assez
 that's enough ça suffit
enquiry desk les renseignements
entrance l'entrée (f)
entrance fee le prix d'entrée
envelope l'enveloppe (f)
 padded envelope l'enveloppe
 matelassée
epileptic épileptique

equipment l'équipement (m)
eraser la gomme
escalator l'escalator (m)
to escape s'échapper
essential indispensable
estate agency l'agence
 immobilière (f)
Euro (unit of currency) l'euro
eurocheque l'eurochèque (m)
Europe l'Europe (f)
European européen(ne)
European Union l'Union
 européenne (f)
eve la veille
 Christmas Eve la veille de Noël
 New Year's Eve la Saint-Sylvestre
even (number) pair(e)
evening le soir
 this evening ce soir
 tomorrow evening demain soir
 in the evening le soir
 7 o'clock in the evening sept
 heures du soir
evening dress (man) la tenue de
 soirée
 (woman) la robe du soir
evening meal le dîner
every chaque
everyone tout le monde
everything tout
everywhere partout
examination l'examen (m)
example: *for example* par example
excellent excellent(e)
except sauf
excess baggage l'excédent de
 bagages (m)
exchange l'échange (m)
to exchange échanger
exchange rate le taux de change
exciting passionnant(e)
excursion l'excursion (f)
excuse: *excuse me!* excusez-moi!
 (to get by) pardon!
exercise l'exercice (m)

e

exercise book le cahier
exhaust pipe le pot d'échappement
exhibition l'exposition (f)
exit la sortie
expensive cher (chère)
expert m/f l'expert(e)
to expire (ticket, passport) expirer
to explain expliquer
explosion l'explosion (f)
to export exporter
express (train) le rapide
express (parcel, etc) en exprès
extension (electrical) la rallonge
extra (additional) supplémentaire ; (more) encore
eye l'œil (m)
  eyes les yeux
eyebrows les sourcils
eye drops les gouttes pour les yeux
eyelashes les cils
eye shadow le fard à paupières

e

F

fabric le tissu
face le visage
face cloth/glove le gant de toilette
facial les soins du visage
facilities les installations
factory l'usine (f)
to faint s'évanouir
fainted évanoui(e)
fair (hair) blond(e)
fair (funfair) la fête foraine
fairway (golf) le fairway
fall (autumn) l'automne (m)
to fall tomber
  he has fallen il est tombé
  she has fallen elle est tombée
family la famille
famous célèbre
fan (handheld) l'éventail (m)
  (electric) le ventilateur

f

(sports) le supporter
fan belt la courroie de ventilateur
far loin
  is it far? c'est loin?
fare (bus, metro, etc) le prix du billet
farm la ferme
farmer le fermier
fashionable à la mode
fast rapide
  too fast trop vite
to fasten (seatbelt) attacher
fat gros (grosse)
father le père
father-in-law le beau-père
fault (defect) un défaut
favourite préféré(e)
fax le fax
  by fax par fax
fax number le numéro de fax
to fax (document) faxer
  (person) envoyer un fax à
feather la plume
February février
to feed nourrir
to feel sentir
  I feel sick j'ai la nausée
feet les pieds
felt-tip pen le feutre
female (animal) la femelle
ferry le ferry
festival le festival
to fetch aller chercher
fever la fièvre
few peu
  a few quelques-un(e)s
fiancé(e) le fiancé/la fiancée
field le champ
fig la figue
file (computer) le fichier
  (for papers) le dossier
to fill remplir
to fill up (with petrol) faire le plein
  fill it up! (car) le plein!

fillet le filet
filling *(in tooth)* le plombage
film le film
  (for camera) la pellicule
  colour film la pellicule couleur
  black and white film la pellicule noir et blanc
Filofax® Filofax®
filter *(on cigarette)* le filtre
  oil filter le filtre à huile
to find trouver
fine *(penalty)* la contravention
finger le doigt
to finish finir
finished fini(e)
fir le sapin
fire le feu ; l'incendie *(m)*
fire brigade les pompiers
fire engine la voiture de pompiers
fire escape *(staircase)* l'échelle de secours *(f)*
fire exit la sortie de secours
fire extinguisher l'extincteur *(m)*
fireplace la cheminée
firework le feu d'artifice
firm la compagnie
first premier(-ière)
  the first train le premier train
first aid les premiers secours
first aid kit la trousse de secours
first-class de première classe
first name le prénom
fish le poisson
to fish pêcher
fisherman le pêcheur
fishing la pêche
  to go fishing aller à la pêche
fishing permit le permis de pêche
fishing rod la canne à pêche
fishmonger's le/la marchand(e) de poisson
fit *(medical)* l'attaque *(f)*
to fit: *it doesn't fit me* ça ne me va pas

to fix *(repair)* réparer
  can you fix it? vous pouvez le réparer?
fizzy gazeux(-euse)
flag le drapeau
flannel *(facecloth)* le gant de toilette
flash *(for camera)* le flash
flashlight la lampe de poche
flask *(vacuum flask)* le Thermos®
flat *(appartment)* l'appartement *(m)*
flat *(level)* plat
  (tyre) dégonflé
  (beer) éventé
flat tyre le pneu dégonflé
flavour le goût
  (of ice cream) le parfum
flaw le défaut
fleas les puces
fleece *(top, jacket)* la laine polaire
flesh la chair
flex *(electrical)* le fil
flight le vol
flip flops les tongs
flippers les palmes
flood l'inondation *(f)*
  flash flood la crue subite
floor *(of room)* le plancher
  (storey) l'étage
  (on the) first floor (au) premier étage
  (on the) ground floor (au) rez-de-chaussée
  (on the) second floor (au) deuxième étage
  which floor? quel étage?
floorcloth la serpillère
floppy disk la disquette
florist's shop le magasin de fleurs
flour la farine
flower la fleur
flu la grippe
fly la mouche
to fly *(person)* aller en avion
  (bird) voler
fly sheet le double toit

f

fog le brouillard
foil le papier alu(minium)
to fold plier
to follow suivre
food la nourriture
food poisoning l'intoxication alimentaire *(f)*
foot le pied
  to go on foot aller à pied
football le football
football match le match de football
football pitch le terrain de football
football player le/la joueur(-euse) de football
footpath le sentier
for pour
  for me/you/us pour moi/vous/nous
  for him/her pour lui/elle

f

forbidden interdit(e)
forecast: *weather forecast* la météo
forehead le front
foreign étranger(-ère)
foreign currency les devises étrangères
forest la forêt
forever toujours
to forget oublier
fork *(for eating)* la fourchette
  (in road) l'embranchement *(m)*
form *(document)* le formulaire ; la fiche
  (shape, style) la forme
fortnight la quinzaine
forward en avant
foul *(football)* la faute
fountain la fontaine

f

fox le renard
fracture la fracture
fragrance le parfum
frame *(picture)* le cadre

France la France
  in/to France en France
free *(not occupied)* libre
  (costing nothing) gratis
freezer le congélateur
French français(e)
  (language) le français
french beans les haricots verts
french fries les frites
French people les Français
frequent fréquent(e)
fresh frais (fraîche)
fresh water *(not salt)* l'eau douce *(f)*
Friday vendredi
fridge le frigo
fried frit(e)
friend *m/f* l'ami(e)
frog la grenouille
frogs' legs les cuisses de grenouille
from de
  I'm from England je suis anglais(e)
  I'm from Scotland je suis écossais(e)
front le devant
  in front of... devant...
front door la porte d'entrée
frost le gel
frozen gelé(e)
  (food) surgelé(e)
fruit le fruit
  dried fruit les fruits secs
fruit juice le jus de fruit
fruit salad la salade de fruits
to fry frire
frying-pan la poêle
fuel le combustible
fuel gauge l'indicateur de niveau d'essence
fuel pump la pompe d'alimentation
fuel tank le réservoir d'essence
full plein(e)
  (occupied) occupé

full board la pension complète
fumes *(exhaust)* les gaz
 d'échappement
fun: to have fun s'amuser
funeral les obsèques
funfair la fête foraine
funny *(amusing)* amusant(e)
fur la fourrure
fur coat le manteau de fourrure
furnished meublé(e)
furniture les meubles
fuse le fusible
fuse box la boîte à fusibles
futon le futon
future l'avenir *(m)*

G

gallery la galerie
gallon = approx. 4.5 litres
game le jeu
 (meat) le gibier
garage le garage
garden le jardin
gardener le jardinier
garlic l'ail *(m)*
gas le gaz
gas cooker la gazinière
gas cylinder la bouteille de gaz
gastritis la gastrite
gate la porte
gay *(person)* homo
gear la vitesse
 in first gear en première
 in second gear en seconde
gearbox la boîte de vitesses
generous généreux(-euse)
gents *(toilet)* les toilettes
genuine authentique
geranium le géranium
German allemand(e)
 (language) l'allemand *(m)*
German measles la rubéole
Germany l'Allemagne *(f)*

to get *(obtain)* obtenir
 (to fetch) aller chercher
to get in *(vehicle)* monter
to get off *(bus, etc)* descendre
gift le cadeau
gift shop la boutique de souvenirs
gin le gin
 gin and tonic le gin-tonic
ginger *(spice)* le gingembre
girl la fille
girlfriend la copine
 my girlfriend ma copine
gîte le gîte
to give donner
to give back rendre
glacier le glacier
glass *(to drink out of)* le verre
glasses *(spectacles)* les lunettes
glasses case l'étui à lunettes *(m)*
gloves les gants
glue la colle
to go aller see **GRAMMAR**
 I'm going to Paris je vais à Paris
 we're going to hire a car nous
 allons louer une voiture
to go back retourner
to go downstairs descendre
to go in entrer
to go out *(leave)* sortir
goat la chèvre
goggles *(for swimming)* les
 lunettes de natation
gold l'or
 is it gold? c'est en or?
golf le golf
golf ball la balle de golf
golf clubs les clubs de golf
golf course le terrain de golf
good bon (bonne)
 (that's) good! (c'est) bien!
good afternoon bonjour
goodbye au revoir
good day bonjour
good evening bonsoir

g

good morning bonjour
good night bonne nuit
goose l'oie (f)
gooseberry la groseille à maquereau
Gothic gothique
gram le gramme
granddaughter la petite-fille
grandfather le grand-père
grandmother la grand-mère
grandparents les grands-parents
grandson le petit-fils
grapefruit le pamplemousse
grapefruit juice le jus de pamplemousse
grapes le raisin
  green grapes les raisins blancs
  black grapes les raisins noirs
grass l'herbe (f)
grated (cheese) râpé(e)
grater la râpe
greasy gras (grasse)

g

great (big) grand(e)
  (wonderful) formidable
Great Britain la Grande-Bretagne
green vert(e)
green card (car insurance) la carte verte
greengrocer's le magasin de fruits et légumes
greetings card la carte de vœux
grey gris(e)
grill (part of cooker) le gril
grilled grillé(e)
grocer's l'épicerie (f)
ground la terre ; le sol
ground floor le rez-de-chaussée
  on the ground floor au rez-de-chaussée
groundsheet le tapis de sol

g

group le groupe
to grow (cultivate) cultiver
guarantee la garantie
guard (on train) le chef de train

guest (house guest) m/f l'invité(e)
  (in hotel) le/la client(e)
guesthouse la pension
guide (tourist guide) le/la guide
guidebook le guide
guided tour la visite guidée
guitar la guitare
gun (rifle) le fusil
  (pistol) le pistolet
gym shoes les chaussures de sport

H

haberdasher's la mercerie
haemorrhoids les hémorroïdes
hail la grêle
hair les cheveux
hairbrush la brosse à cheveux
haircut la coupe (de cheveux)
hairdresser le/la coiffeur(-euse)
hairdryer le sèche-cheveux
hair dye la teinture pour les cheveux
hair gel le gel pour cheveux
hairgrip la pince à cheveux
hair mousse la mousse coiffante
hair spray la laque
half la moitié
  half an hour une demi-heure
half board la demi-pension
half fare le demi-tarif
half-price à moitié prix
ham (cooked) le jambon
  (cured) le jambon cru
hamburger le hamburger
hammer le marteau
hand la main
handbag le sac à main
hand luggage les bagages à main
hand-made fait main
handicapped handicapé(e)
handkerchief le mouchoir
handle la poignée

handlebars le guidon
handsome beau (belle)
hanger (coathanger) le cintre
hangover la gueule de bois
to hang up (telephone) raccrocher
hang-gliding le deltaplane
  to go hang-gliding faire du deltaplane
to happen arriver ; se passer
  what happened? qu'est-ce qui s'est passé?
happy heureux(-euse)
  happy birthday! bon anniversaire!
harbour le port
hard (not soft) dur(e)
  (not easy) difficile
hard disk le disque dur
hardware shop la quincaillerie
hare le lièvre
to harm someone faire du mal à quelqu'un
harvest (grape) les vendanges
hat le chapeau
to have avoir *see* GRAMMAR
to have to devoir *see* GRAMMAR
hay fever le rhume des foins
hazelnut la noisette
he il *see* GRAMMAR
head la tête
headache le mal de tête
  I have a headache j'ai mal à la tête
headlights les phares
headphones les écouteurs
head waiter le maître d'hôtel
health food shop la boutique de produits diététiques
to hear entendre
hearing aid la prothèse auditive
heart le cœur
heart attack la crise cardiaque
heartburn les brûlures d'estomac
heater l'appareil de chauffage (m)
heating le chauffage
to heat up faire chauffer

heaven le paradis
heavy lourd(e)
heel le talon
height la hauteur
helicopter l'hélicoptère (m)
hello bonjour!
  (on telephone) allô?
helmet le casque
help! au secours!
to help aider
  can you help me? vous pouvez m'aider?
hem l'ourlet (m)
hen la poule
hepatitis l'hépatite (f)
her son/sa/ses *see* GRAMMAR
  her passport son passeport
  her room sa chambre
  her suitcases ses valises
herb l'herbe (f)
herb tea la tisane
here ici
  here is... voici...
  here is my passport voici mon passeport
hernia la hernie
hi! salut!
to hide (something) cacher
  (oneself) se cacher
high haut(e)
high blood pressure la tension
high chair la chaise haute
high tide la marée haute
hill la colline
hill-walking la randonnée (de basse montagne)
him il ; lui *see* GRAMMAR
hip la hanche
  hip replacement la pose d'une prothèse de la hanche
hire la location
  car hire la location de voitures
  bike hire la location de bicyclettes
  boat hire la location de bateaux
  ski hire la location de skis

h

to hire louer
hired car la voiture de location
his son/sa/ses *see* **GRAMMAR**
  his passport son passeport
  his room sa chambre
  his suitcases ses valises
historic historique
history l'histoire *(f)*
to hit frapper
to hitchhike faire du stop
HIV le VIH
hobby le passe-temps
to hold tenir
  (contain) contenir
hold-up *(traffic jam)*
  l'embouteillage *(m)*
hole le trou
holiday les vacances
  on holiday en vacances
home la maison
  at my/your/our chez moi/vous/
  nous
homeopathy l'homéopathie *(f)*
homesick: to be homesick avoir
  le mal du pays
  I'm homesick j'ai le mal du pays
homosexual homosexuel(le)
honest honnête
honey le miel
honeymoon la lune de miel
hood *(of car)* le capot
hook *(fishing)* l'hameçon *(m)*
to hope espérer
  I hope so/not j'espère que
  oui/non
hors d'œuvre le hors d'œuvre
horse le cheval
horse-riding: to go horse-riding
  faire du cheval
hosepipe le tuyau d'arrosage
hospital l'hôpital *(m)*
hostel *(youth hostel)* l'auberge de
  jeunesse *(f)*
hot chaud(e)
  I'm hot j'ai chaud

  it's hot (weather) il fait chaud
hot chocolate le chocolat chaud
hot water l'eau chaude
hot-water bottle la bouillotte
hotel l'hôtel *(m)*
hour l'heure *(f)*
  half an hour une demi-heure
house la maison
househusband l'homme au
  foyer *(m)*
housewife la femme au foyer
house wine le vin en pichet
hovercraft l'aéroglisseur *(m)*
how? *(in what way)* comment?
  how much/many? combien?
  how are you? comment allez-
  vous?
hundred cent
  five hundred cinq cents
hungry: to be hungry avoir faim
  I'm hungry j'ai faim
to hunt chasser
hunting permit le permis de
  chasse
hurry: I'm in a hurry je suis pressé
to hurt: that hurts ça fait mal
  my back/arm hurts j'ai mal au
  dos/bras
  my head hurts j'ai mal à la tête
husband le mari
hut *(bathing/beach)* la cabine
  (mountain) le refuge
hydrofoil l'hydrofoil *(m)*
hypodermic needle l'aiguille
  hypodermique *(f)*

I

I je *see* **GRAMMAR**
ice la glace
  (cube) le glaçon
  with ice avec glaçons
icecream la glace
ice lolly l'esquimau *(m)*
ice rink la patinoire

to ice skate faire du patin (à glace)
ice skates les patins (à glace)
idea l'idée (f)
identity card la carte d'identité
if si
ignition l'allumage (m)
ill malade
illness la maladie
immediately immédiatement
immersion heater le chauffe-eau électrique
immunisation l'immunisation (f)
to import importer
important important(e)
impossible impossible
to improve améliorer
in dans
  in 2 hours' time dans deux heures
  in France en France
  in Canada au Canada
  in London à Londres
in front of devant
inch = approx. 2.5 cm
included compris(e)
inconvenient gênant
to increase augmenter
indicator (car) le clignotant
indigestion l'indigestion (f)
indigestion tablets les comprimés contre les troubles digestifs
indoors à l'intérieur
infection l'infection (f)
infectious infectieux(-euse)
information les renseignements
ingredients les ingrédients
inhaler l'inhalateur (m)
injection la piqûre
to injure blesser
injured blessé(e)
injury la blessure
inn l'auberge (f)
inner tube la chambre à air
insect l'insecte (m)
insect bite la piqûre (d'insecte)

insect repellent le produit pour éloigner les insectes
inside à l'intérieur
instant coffee le café instantané
instead of au lieu de
instructor le moniteur/la monitrice
insulin l'insuline (f)
insurance l'assurance (f)
insurance certificate l'attestation d'assurance (f)
insured assuré(e)
intelligent intelligent(e)
to intend to avoir l'intention de
interesting intéressant(e)
international international(e)
internet l'internet (m)
  internet café le cybercafé
interpreter l'interprète (m/f)
interval (theatre) l'entracte (m)
interview l'entrevue (f)
  (TV, etc) l'interview (f)
into dans ; en
  into town en ville
to introduce présenter
invitation l'invitation (f)
to invite inviter
invoice la facture
Ireland l'Irlande (f)
Irish irlandais(e)
iron (for clothes) le fer à repasser
  (metal) le fer
to iron repasser
ironing board la planche à repasser
ironmonger's la quincaillerie
is see (to be) GRAMMAR
island l'île (f)
it il ; elle see GRAMMAR
Italian italien(ne)
Italy l'Italie (f)
to itch démanger
  it itches ça me démange
item l'article (m)
itemized bill la facture détaillée
ivory l'ivoire (m)

J

jack *(for car)* le cric
jacket la veste
  waterproof jacket l'anorak *(m)*
jacuzzi le jacuzzi
jam *(food)* la confiture
jammed *(stuck)* coincé(e)
January janvier
Japan le Japon
jar *(honey, jam, etc)* le pot
jaundice la jaunisse
jaw la mâchoire
jazz le jazz
jealous jaloux(-ouse)
jeans le jean
jellyfish la méduse
jet ski le jet-ski
jetty *(landing pier)* l'embarcadère *(m)*
Jew le Juif/la Juive
jeweller's la bijouterie
jewellery les bijoux
Jewish juif (juive)
job le travail ; l'emploi
to jog faire du jogging
to join *(become member)* s'inscrire
joint *(body)* l'articulation *(f)*
to joke plaisanter
joke la plaisanterie
journalist le/la journaliste
journey le voyage
judge le juge
jug le pichet
juice le jus
  fruit juice le jus de fruit
  orange juice le jus d'orange
July juillet
to jump sauter
jumper le pull
jump leads les câbles de raccordement pour batterie
junction *(road)* le croisement ; le carrefour

June juin
just: *just two* deux seulement
  I've just arrived je viens d'arriver

K

karaoke le karaoke
to keep *(retain)* garder
kennel la niche
kettle la bouilloire
key la clé
  the car key la clé de la voiture
keyboard le clavier
keyring le porte-clés
kid *(goat)* le chevreau
  (child) le gosse
kidneys *(as food)* les rognons
kill tuer
kilo(gram) le kilo
kilometre le kilomètre
kind *(person)* gentil(-ille)
king le roi
kiss le baiser
to kiss embrasser
kitchen la cuisine
kitchen paper l'essuie-tout *(m)*
kitten le chaton
knee le genou
knickers la culotte
knife le couteau
to knock *(on door)* frapper
to knock down *(in car)* renverser
to knock over *(vase, glass, etc)* faire tomber
knot le nœud
to know *(be aware of)* savoir
  (person, place) connaître
  I don't know je ne sais pas
  I don't know Paris je ne connais pas Paris
to know how to do sth savoir faire quelque chose
  to know how to swim savoir nager
kosher kascher

L

label l'étiquette *(f)*
lace la dentelle
laces *(for shoes)* les lacets
ladder l'échelle *(f)*
ladies *(toilet)* les toilettes pour dames
lady la dame
lager la bière
  bottled lager la bière bouteille
  draught lager la bière pression
lake le lac
lamb l'agneau *(m)*
lamp la lampe
land la terre
landlady *(of flat, etc)* la propriétaire
landlord *(of flat, etc)* le propriétaire
landslide le glissement de terrain
lane la ruelle
  (of motorway) la voie
language la langue
laptop le portable
large grand(e)
last dernier(-ière)
  last month le mois dernier
  last night *(evening/night-time)* hier soir ; la nuit dernière
  last time la dernière fois
  last week la semaine dernière
  last year l'année dernière
  the last bus le dernier bus
  the last trian le dernier train
late tard
  the train is late le train a du retard
  sorry we are late excusez-nous d'arriver en retard
later plus tard
to laugh rire
launderette la laverie automatique
laundry service le service de blanchisserie
lavatory les toilettes
law la loi

lawyer *m/f* l'avocat(e)
laxative le laxatif
layby l'aire de stationnement *(f)*
lead *(metal)* le plomb
lead-free petrol l'essence sans plomb *(m)*
lead *(electric)* le fil
leaf la feuille
leak la fuite
to leak: *it's leaking* il y a une fuite
to learn apprendre
leather le cuir
to leave *(depart for)* partir
  (depart from) quitter
  (to leave behind) laisser
  to leave for Paris partir pour Paris
  to leave London quitter Londres
leek le poireau
left: *on/to the left* à gauche
left-luggage *(office)* la consigne
left-handed *(person)* gaucher(-ère)
leg la jambe
legal légal(e)
leggings le collant
leisure centre le centre de loisirs
lemon le citron
lemonade la limonade
lemon tea le thé au citron
to lend prêter
length la longueur
lens *(of camera, etc)* l'objectif *(m)*
  (contact lens) la lentille
Lent le Carême
lentils les lentilles
lesbian la lesbienne
less moins
  less than moins de
lesson la leçon
to let *(allow)* permettre
  (to hire out) louer
letter la lettre
letterbox la boîte à lettres
lettuce la laitue
level crossing le passage à niveau

library la bibliothèque
licence le permis
lid le couvercle
life belt la bouée de sauvetage
lifeboat le canot de sauvetage
lifeguard le surveillant de plage
life insurance l'assurance-vie *(f)*
life jacket le gilet de sauvetage
life raft le radeau de sauvetage
lift *(elevator)* l'ascenseur *(m)*
lift pass *(on ski slopes)* le forfait
light *(not heavy)* léger(-ère)
light la lumière
　have you got a light? avez-vous
　du feu?
light bulb l'ampoule *(f)*
lighter le briquet
lighthouse le phare
lightning les éclairs
　a flash of lightning un éclair
like *(preposition)* comme
　like this comme ça
to like aimer
　I like coffee j'aime le café
　I don't like coffee je n'aime pas
　le café
　I'd like... je voudrais...
　we'd like... nous voudrions...
lilo® le matelas pneumatique
lime *(fruit)* le citron vert
linen le lin
lingerie la lingerie
lion le lion
lip la lèvre
lip-reading lire sur les lèvres
lip salve le baume pour les lèvres
lipstick le rouge à lèvres
liqueur la liqueur
list la liste
to listen to écouter
litre le litre
litter *(rubbish)* les ordures
little petit(e)
　a little... un peu de...

to live *(in a place)* vivre ; habiter
　I live in London j'habite à
　Londres
　he lives in a flat il habite un
　appartement
liver le foie
living room le salon
loaf le pain
lobster le homard
local local(e)
lock la serrure
　the lock is broken la serrure est
　cassée
to lock fermer à clé
locker *(for luggage)* le casier
log *(for fire)* la bûche
lollipop la sucette
London Londres
　to/in London à Londres
long long(ue)
　for a long time longtemps
long sighted hypermétrope
to look after garder
to look at regarder
to look for chercher
loose *(not fastened)* desserré(e)
lorry le camion
to lose perdre
lost *(object)* perdu(e)
　I've lost... j'ai perdu...
　I'm lost je suis perdu(e)
lost property office le bureau
　des objets trouvés
lot: *a lot of* beaucoup de
lotion la lotion
lottery la loterie
loud fort(e)
lounge *(in hotel, airport)* le salon
love l'amour
to love *(person)* aimer
　I love you je t'aime
　(food, activity, etc) adorer
　I love swimming j'adore nager
lovely beau (belle)
low bas (basse)

to lower baisser
low-fat allégé(e)
low tide la marée basse
luck la chance
lucky chanceux(-euse)
luggage les bagages
  hand luggage les bagages à main
luggage allowance le poids
  maximum autorisé
luggage rack le porte-bagages
luggage tag l'étiquette à
  bagages *(f)*
luggage trolley le chariot (à
  bagages)
lump *(swelling)* la bosse
lunch le déjeuner
lung le poumon
luxury: *de luxe* de luxe

M

machine la machine
magazine la revue
maggot l'asticot
magnet l'aimant *(m)*
magnifying glass la loupe
maid la domestique
maiden name le nom de jeune fille
mail le courrier
  by mail par la poste
main principal(e)
main course *(of meal)* le plat
  principal
mains *(electricity, water)* le secteur
major road la route principale
to make faire
make-up le maquillage
male *(person)* masculin
mallet le maillet
man l'homme *(m)*
to manage *(to be in charge of)* gérer
manager le/la directeur(-trice)
man-made *(fibre)* synthétique
manual *(car)* manuel(le)

many beaucoup de
map la carte
  road map la carte routière
  street map le plan de la ville
March mars
margarine la margarine
marina la marina
marinade la marinade
marjoram la marjolaine
mark *(stain)* la tache
market le marché
  where is the market? où est le
  marché
  when is the market? le marché,
  c'est quel jour?
marmalade la marmelade
  d'oranges
married marié(e)
  I'm married je suis marié(e)
  are you married? vous êtes
  marié(e)?
marrow *(vegetable)* la courge
marsh le marais
marzipan la pâte d'amandes
mascara le mascara
mass *(in church)* la messe
masterpiece le chef-d'œuvre
mast le mât
match *(game)* la partie
matches les allumettes
material *(cloth)* le tissu
to matter: *it doesn't matter* ça
  ne fait rien
  what's the matter? qu'est-ce
  qu'il y a?
mattress le matelas .
May mai
mayonnaise la mayonnaise
mayor le maire
me moi *see* GRAMMAR
meadow le pré
meal le repas
measles la rougeole

m

to measure mesurer
meat la viande
  red meat la viande rouge
  white meat la viande blanche
  I don't eat meat je ne mange pas de viande
mechanic le mécanicien
medical insurance l'assurance maladie *(f)*
medical treatment les soins médicaux
medicine le médicament
Mediterranean Sea la Méditérranée
medium rare *(meat)* à point
to meet rencontrer
meeting la réunion
melon le melon
  watermelon la pastèque
to melt fondre
member *(of club, etc)* le membre
memory la mémoire

m

men les hommes
to mend réparer
meningitis la méningite
menu *(choices)* le menu
  (card) la carte
message le message
metal le métal
meter le compteur
metre le mètre
metro le métro
  metro station la station de métro
microwave oven le four à micro-ondes
midday midi
  at midday à midi
middle-aged d'un certain âge
midge le moucheron
midnight minuit
  at midnight à minuit

m

migraine la migraine
  I have a migraine j'ai la migraine
mile 5 miles = approx. 8 km
milk le lait

baby milk (formula) le lait maternisé
fresh milk le lait frais
full cream milk le lait entier
hot milk le lait chaud
long-life milk le lait longue conservation
powdered milk le lait en poudre
(semi-)skimmed milk le lait (demi-)écrémé
soya milk le lait de soja
UHT milk le lait UHT
with milk au lait
milkshake le milk-shake
millimetre le millimètre
million le million
mince *(meat)* la viande hachée
to mind: *do you mind if I...?* ça vous gêne si je...?
  I don't mind ça m'est égal
  do you mind? vous permettez?
mineral water l'eau minérale *(f)*
minister *(church)* le pasteur
minor road la route secondaire
mint *(herb)* la menthe
  (sweet) le bonbon à la menthe
minute la minute
mirror la glace
  (in car) le rétroviseur
miscarriage la fausse couche
to miss *(train, flight, etc)* rater
Miss Mademoiselle
missing *(disappeared)* disparu(e)
mistake l'erreur *(f)*
misty brumeux(-euse)
misunderstanding le malentendu
mobile phone le (téléphone) portable
modem le modem
modern moderne
moisturizer la crème hydratante
mole *(on skin)* le grain de beauté
moment: *at the moment* en ce moment
monastery le monastère

Monday lundi
money l'argent *(m)*
  I have no money je n'ai pas
  d'argent
moneybelt la ceinture
  porte-monnaie
money order le mandat
monkey le singe
month le mois
  this month ce mois-ci
  last month le mois dernier
  next month le mois prochain
monthly mensuel(-elle)
monument le monument
moon la lune
mop *(for floor)* le balai à laver
more encore
  more wine plus de vin
more than plus de
  more than 3 plus de trois
morning le matin
  in the morning le matin
  this morning ce matin
  tomorrow morning demain matin
mosque la mosquée
mosquito le moustique
mosquito bite la piqûre de
  moustique
mosquito coil la spirale
  anti-moustiques
mosquito net la moustiquaire
mosquito repellent le produit
  pour éloigner les moustiques
moth *(clothes)* la mite
mother la mère
mother-in-law la belle-mère
motor le moteur
motorbike la moto
motor boat le bateau à moteur
motorway l'autoroute *(f)*
mountain la montagne
mountain bike le VTT (vélo
  tout-terrain)
mountain rescue le sauvetage en
  montagne

mountaineering l'alpinisme *(m)*
mouse *(animal, computer)* la souris
mousse la mousse
moustache la moustache
mouth la bouche
mouthwash l'eau dentifrice *(f)*
Mr Monsieur
Mrs Madame
Ms Madame
much beaucoup
  too much trop
mud la boue
mug: *I've been mugged* je me
  suis fait agresser
mugging l'agression *(f)*
mumps les oreillons
muscle le muscle
museum le musée
mushroom le champignon
music la musique
musical *(show)* la comédie musicale
mussel la moule
must devoir
  I must... je dois...
mustard la moutarde
mutton le mouton
my mon/ma/mes *see* **GRAMMAR**
  my passport mon passeport
  my room ma chambre
  my suitcases mes valises

N

nail *(metal)* le clou
  (finger) l'ongle *(m)*
nailbrush la brosse à ongles
nail clippers le coupe-ongles
nail file la lime à ongles
nail polish le vernis à ongles
nail polish remover le dissolvant
nail scissors les ciseaux à ongles
name le nom
  my name is... je m'appelle...
  what is your name? comment
  vous appelez-vous?

n

nanny le/la baby-sitter
napkin la serviette de table
nappy la couche
narrow étroit(e)
national national(e)
nationality la nationalité
national park le parc national
natural naturel(le)
nature reserve la réserve naturelle
nature trail le sentier de grande randonnée
navy blue bleu marine
near près de
 near the bank près de la banque
 is it near? c'est près d'ici?
necessary nécessaire
neck le cou
necklace le collier
nectarine le brugnon
to need (to) avoir besoin de
 I need... /we need... j'ai besoin de... /nous avons besoin de...
 I need a phone j'ai besoin d'un téléphone
 I need to phone j'ai besoin de téléphoner
needle l'aiguille *(f)*
 a needle and thread du fil et une aiguille
negative *(photography)* le négatif
neighbour le/la voisin(e)
nephew le neveu
nest le nid
net le filet
never jamais
 I never drink wine je ne bois jamais de vin
new nouveau(-elle)
news *(TV, radio, etc)* les informations
newspaper le journal
news stand le kiosque
New Year le Nouvel An
 happy New Year! bonne année!
New Year's Eve la Saint-Sylvestre

New Zealand la Nouvelle-Zélande
next prochain(e)
 (after) ensuite
 the next train le prochain train
 next month le mois prochain
 next week la semaine prochaine
 next Monday lundi prochain
 next to à côté de
 we're going to Paris next ensuite nous allons à Paris
nice beau (belle)
 (enjoyable) bon (bonne)
 (person) sympathique
 have a nice time! amuse-toi bien!
niece la nièce
night *(night-time)* la nuit
 (evening) le soir
 at night la nuit/le soir
 last night hier soir
 tomorrow night (evening) demain soir
 tonight ce soir
nightclub la boîte de nuit
nightdress la chemise de nuit
no non
 (without) sans
 no problem pas de problème
 no thanks non merci
 no ice sans glaçons
 no sugar sans sucre
nobody personne
noise le bruit
 it's very noisy il y a beaucoup de bruit
non-alcoholic sans alcool
none aucun(e)
non-smoker: *I'm a non-smoker* je ne fume pas
north le nord
Northern Ireland l'Irlande du Nord *(f)*
North Sea la mer du Nord
nose le nez
not pas
 I am not... je ne suis pas...

note (banknote) le billet
  (letter) la note
nothing rien
notice (warning) l'avis (m)
  (sign) le panneau
noun le nom
novel le roman
November novembre
now maintenant
nuclear nucléaire
number (quantity) le nombre
  (of room, house) le numéro
  phone number le numéro de
  téléphone
numberplate (of car) la plaque
  d'immatriculation
nurse m/f l'infirmier/l'infirmière
nursery school l'école maternelle (f)
nursery slope la piste pour
  débutants
nut (to eat) la noix
  (for bolt) l'écrou (m)

O

oar l'aviron (m) ; la rame
oats l'avoine (f)
to obtain obtenir
occupation (work) l'emploi (m)
ocean l'océan (m)
October octobre
odd (number) impair(e)
of de
  a glass of... un verre de...
  made of... en...
off (light) éteint(e)
  (rotten) mauvais(e) ; pourri(e)
office le bureau
often souvent
oil (for car, food) l'huile (f)
oil filter le filtre à huile
oil gauge la jauge de niveau
  d'huile
ointment la pommade
OK! (agreed) d'accord!

old vieux (vieille)
  how old are you? quel âge
  avez-vous?
  I'm... years old j'ai... ans
olive l'olive (f)
olive oil l'huile d'olive (f)
omelette l'omelette (f)
on (light) allumé(e)
  (engine, etc) en marche
  on the table sur la table
  on time à l'heure
once une fois
  at once tout de suite
one un/une
one-way (street) à sens unique
onion l'oignon (m)
only seulement
open ouvert(e)
to open ouvrir
opera l'opéra (m)
operation (surgical) l'opération (f)
operator (telephone) le/la
  standardiste
opposite en face de
  opposite the bank en face de la
  banque
optician l'opticien/l'opticienne
or ou
  tea or coffee? thé ou café?
orange (fruit) l'orange
  (colour) orange
orange juice le jus d'orange
orchard le verger
orchestra l'orchestre (m)
order (in restaurant) la commande
  out of order en panne
to order (in restaurant) commander
organic biologique
to organize organiser
other autre
ounce = approx. 30 g
our (sing) notre
  (plural) nos *see* GRAMMAR
  notre passeport our passport
  notre chambre our room
  nos valises our suitcases

O

out *(light)* éteint(e)
  he's/she's out il/elle est sorti(e)
outdoor *(pool, etc)* en plein air
outside dehors
oven le four
over *(on top of)* au-dessus de
to overbook faire du surbooking
to overcharge faire payer trop cher
overdone *(food)* trop cuit(e)
overdose la surdose
to overheat surchauffer
to overload surcharger
to oversleep se réveiller en retard
to overtake *(in car)* doubler ; dépasser
to owe devoir
  you owe me... vous me devez...
owl le hibou ; la chouette
to own posséder
owner le/la propriétaire
oyster l'huître *(f)*

P

pacemaker le stimulateur (cardiaque)
to pack *(luggage)* faire les bagages
package le paquet
package tour le voyage organisé
packet le paquet
padded envelope l'enveloppe matelassée
paddling pool la pataugeoire
padlock le cadenas
page la page
paid payé(e)
  I've paid j'ai payé
pain la douleur
painful douloureux(-euse)
painkiller l'analgésique *(m)*
to paint peindre
painting *(picture)* le tableau
pair la paire
palace le palais

pale pâle
pan *(saucepan)* la casserole
  (frying pan) la poêle
pancake la crêpe
panniers *(for bike)* les sacoches
pants *(underwear)* le slip
panties la culotte
panty liner le protège-slip
paper le papier
paper napkins les serviettes en papier
paracetamol le paracétamol
paraffin le kérosène
paralysed paralysé(e)
parcel le colis
pardon? comment?
  I beg your pardon! pardon!
parents les parents
Paris Paris
park le parc
to park garer (la voiture)
parking disk le disque de stationnement
parking meter le parcmètre
parking ticket le p.-v.
parmesan le parmesan
parsley le persil
parsnip le panais
part: spare parts les pièces de rechange
partner *(business) m/f* l'associé(e)
  (boy/girlfriend) le compagnon/la compagne
party *(group)* le groupe
  (celebration) la fête ; la soirée
  (political) le parti
pass *(bus, train)* la carte
  (mountain) le col
passenger le passager/la passagère
passport le passeport
  my passport mon passeport
passport control le contrôle des passeports
pasta les pâtes

pastry la pâte
  (cake) la pâtisserie
pâté le pâté
path le chemin
patience *(card game)* la réussite
patient *(in hospital)* le/la patient(e)
pavement le trottoir
to pay payer
  I'd like to pay je voudrais payer
  where do I pay? où est-ce qu'il faut payer?
payment le paiement
payphone le téléphone public
peace *(after war)* la paix
peach la pêche
peak rate le plein tarif
peanut la cacahuète
  peanut butter le beurre de cacahuètes
pear la poire
peas les petits pois
pedal la pédale
pedestrian le/la piéton(ne)
pedestrian crossing le passage clouté
to peel *(fruit)* peler
peg *(for clothes)* la pince à linge
  (for tent) le piquet
pen le stylo
pencil le crayon
penfriend le/la correspondant(e)
penicillin la pénicilline
peninsula la péninsule
penis le pénis
penknife le canif
pensioner le/la retraité(e)
pepper *(spice)* le poivre
  (vegetable) le poivron
per par
  per day par jour
  per hour à l'heure
  per person par personne
  per week par semaine
  100 km per hour 100 km à l'heure

perch *(fish)* la perche
perfect parfait(e)
performance *(show)* le spectacle
perfume le parfum
perhaps peut-être
period *(menstruation)* les règles
perm la permanente
permit le permis
person la personne
personal organizer *(Filofax)* l'agenda *(m)*
personal stereo le baladeur
pet l'animal de compagnie
petrol l'essence *(f)*
  4-star petrol le super *(f)*
  unleaded petrol l'essence sans plomb
petrol cap le bouchon de réservoir
petrol pump la pompe à essence
petrol station la station-service
petrol tank le réservoir
pharmacy la pharmacie
phone le téléphone
  by phone par téléphone
to phone téléphoner
phonebook l'annuaire *(m)*
phonebox la cabine (téléphonique)
phone call l'appel *(m)*
phonecard la télécarte
photocopy la photocopie
to photocopy photocopier
photograph la photo
  to take a photograph prendre une photo
phrase book le guide de conversation
piano le piano
pickpocket le pickpocket
picnic le pique-nique
  to have a picnic pique-niquer
picnic rug le plaid
picture *(painting)* le tableau
  (photo) la photo
pie *(savoury)* la tourte

p

piece le morceau
pier la jetée
pig le cochon
pill la pilule
  I'm on the pill je prends la pilule
pillow l'oreiller (m)
pillowcase la taie d'oreiller
pilot le pilote
pin l'épingle (f)
pine le pin
pineapple l'ananas (m)
pink rose
pint = approx. 0.5 litre
  a pint of... un demi-litre de...
pipe (for water, gas) le tuyau
  (smoking) la pipe
pistachio la pistache
pizza la pizza
plain (unflavoured) ordinaire
plait la natte
plan (map) le plan

p

plant (in garden) la plante
plane (aircraft) l'avion (m)
plaster (sticking plaster) le
  sparadrap
  (for broken limb, on wall) le plâtre
plastic (made of) en plastique
plastic bag le sac en plastique
plate l'assiette (f)
platform (railway) le quai
  which platform? quel quai?
play (at theatre) la pièce
to play (games) jouer
play area l'aire de jeux
playroom la salle de jeux
pleasant agréable
please s'il vous plaît
pleased content(e)
  pleased to meet you!
  enchanté(e)!

p

pliers la pince
plug (electrical) la prise
  (for sink) la bonde
plum la prune

plumber le plombier
plunger (to clear sink) le
  débouchoir à ventouse
pocket la poche
poem le poème
points (in car) les vis platinées
poison le poison
poisonous vénéneux
police (force) la police
policeman le policier
  (police woman) la femme policier
police station le commissariat ; la
  gendarmerie
polish (for shoes) le cirage
pollen le pollen
polluted pollué(e)
pony le poney
pony-trekking la randonnée à
  cheval
pool (swimming) la piscine
poor pauvre
popcorn le pop-corn
pope le pape
pop socks les mi-bas
popular populaire
pork le porc
port (seaport) le port
  (wine) le porto
porter (for luggage) le porteur
portion la portion
portrait le portrait
Portugal le Portugal
Portuguese portugais(e)
possible possible
post (letters) le courrier
  by post par courrier
to post poster
postbox la boîte aux lettres
postcard la carte postale
postcode le code postal
postman/woman le facteur/la
  factrice
post office la poste
to postpone remettre à plus tard
pot (for cooking) la casserole

potato la pomme de terre
 boiled potatoes les pommes vapeur
 fried potatoes les pommes frites
 mashed potatoes la purée
 roast potatoes les pommes de terre rôties
potato salad la salade de pommes de terre
pothole le nid de poule
pottery la poterie
pound *(money)* la livre
 (weight) = approx. 0.5 kilo
to pour verser
powder la poudre
powdered milk le lait en poudre
power cut la coupure de courant
pram le landau
prawn la crevette
to pray prier
to prefer préférer
pregnant enceinte
 I'm pregnant je suis enceinte
to prepare préparer
prescription l'ordonnance *(f)*
present *(gift)* le cadeau
preservative conservateur *(m)*
pressure la pression
 tyre pressure la pression des pneus
pretty joli(e)
price le prix
price list le tarif
priest le prêtre
prince le prince
princess la princesse
print *(photo)* la photo
private privé(e)
prize le prix
probably probablement
problem le problème
professor le professeur d'université
programme *(TV, etc)* l'émission *(f)*
prohibited interdit(e)

to promise promettre
to pronounce prononcer
 how's it pronounced? comment ça se prononce?
Protestant protestant(e)
to provide fournir
public public(-que)
public holiday le jour férié
pudding le dessert
puff pastry la pâte feuilletée
to pull tirer
 to pull a muscle se faire une élongation
pullover le pull
pump la pompe
pumpkin le potiron
puncture la crevaison
puppet la marionnette
puppet show le spectacle de marionnettes
puppy le chiot
purple violet(-ette)
purpose: on purpose exprès
purse le porte-monnaie
to push pousser
pushchair la poussette
to put *(place)* mettre
pyjamas le pyjama
Pyrenees les Pyrénées

Q

quality la qualité
quantity la quantité
quarantine la quarantaine
quarter le quart
quay le quai
queen la reine
question la question
to queue faire la queue
quick rapide
quickly vite
quiet *(place)* tranquille
quilt la couette

q

quite *(rather)* assez
(completely) complètement
quite good pas mal
it's quite expensive c'est assez cher
quiz le jeu-concours

R

rabbit le lapin
rabies la rage
race *(people)* la race
(sport) la course
racket la raquette
radiator le radiateur
radio la radio
radish le radis
railway le chemin de fer
railway station la gare
rain la pluie
to rain: *it's raining* il pleut
raincoat l'imperméable *(m)*
raisin le raisin sec
rake le râteau
rape le viol
to rape violer
rare *(uncommon)* rare
(steak) saignant(e)
rash *(skin)* la rougeur
raspberries les framboises
rate *(price)* le tarif
rate of exchange le taux de change
rave *(party)* la rave
raw cru(e)
razor le rasoir
razor blades les lames de rasoir
to read lire
ready prêt(e)
real vrai(e)
rearview mirror le rétroviseur
receipt le reçu
receiver *(of phone)* le récepteur
recently récemment
reception *(desk)* la réception

receptionist le/la réceptionniste
to recharge *(battery, etc)* recharger
recipe la recette
to recognize reconnaître
to recommend recommander
record *(music)* le disque
to recover *(from illness)* se remettre
red rouge
to reduce réduire
reduction la réduction
reel *(fishing)* le moulinet
referee l'arbitre *(m)*
refill la recharge
to refund rembourser
to refuse refuser
region la région
registered *(letter)* recommandé(e)
to reimburse rembourser
relation *(family)* le/la parent(e)
to remain rester
remember se rappeler
I don't remember je ne m'en souviens pas
remote control la télécommande
to remove enlever
rent le loyer
to rent louer
rental la location
repair la réparation
to repair réparer
to repeat répéter
request la demande
to require avoir besoin de
to rescue sauver
reservation la réservation
to reserve réserver
reserved réservé(e)
resident *m/f* l'habitant(e)
resort *(seaside)* la station balnéaire
ski resort la station de ski
rest *(relaxation)* le repos
(remainder) le reste
to rest se reposer
restaurant le restaurant

restaurant car le wagon-restaurant
retired retraité(e)
to return *(to a place)* retourner
(to return something) rendre
return ticket le billet aller-retour
to reverse faire marche arrière
to reverse the charges appeler
en PCV
reverse-charge call l'appel en
PCV *(m)*
reverse gear la marche arrière
rheumatism le rhumatisme
rhubarb la rhubarbe
rib la côte
ribbon le ruban
rice le riz
rich *(person, food)* riche
to ride *(horse)* faire du cheval
right *(correct)* exact(e)
right la droite
on/to the right à droite
right of way la priorité
ring *(on finger)* la bague
to ring *(bell)* sonner
it's ringing (phone) ça sonne
to ring sb (phone) téléphoner à
quelqu'un
ring road le périphérique
ripe mûr(e)
river la rivière
Riviera *(French)* la Côte d'Azur
road la route
road map la carte routière
road sign le panneau
roadworks les travaux
roast rôti(e)
roll *(bread)* le petit pain
roller blades les patins en ligne
romance *(novel)* le roman d'amour
Romanesque roman(e)
romantic romantique
roof le toit
roof-rack la galerie
room *(in house)* la pièce

(in hotel) la chambre
(space) la place
double room la chambre pour
deux personnes
family room la chambre pour
une famille
single room la chambre pour
une personne
room number le numéro de
chambre
room service le service des
chambres
root la racine
rope la corde
rose la rose
rosé wine le rosé
rotten *(fruit, etc)* pourri(e)
rough: *rough sea* la mer agitée
round rond(e)
roundabout *(traffic)* le rond-point
route la route ; l'itinéraire *(m)*
rowing *(sport)* l'aviron *(m)*
rowing boat la barque
rubber *(material)* le caoutchouc
(eraser) la gomme
rubber band l'élastique *(m)*
rubber gloves les gants en
caoutchouc
rubbish les ordures
rubella la rubéole
rucksack le sac à dos
rug *(carpet)* le tapis
ruins les ruines
ruler *(for measuring)* la règle
rum le rhum
to run courir
rush hour l'heure de pointe *(f)*
rusty rouillé(e)

S

sad triste
saddle la selle
safe *(for valuables)* le coffre-fort

safe sûr ; sans danger
  is it safe? ce n'est pas
  dangereux?
safety belt la ceinture de sécurité
safety pin l'épingle de sûreté *(f)*
sail la voile
sailboard la planche à voile
sailing *(sport)* la voile
sailing boat le voilier
saint le/la saint(e)
salad la salade
  green salad la salade verte
  mixed salad la salade composée
  potato salad la salade de
  pommes de terre
  tomato salad la salade de
  tomates
salad dressing la vinaigrette
salami le salami
salary le salaire
sale la vente
sales *(reductions)* les soldes
salesman/woman le vendeur/la
  vendeuse
sales rep le/la représentant(e)
salmon le saumon
  smoked salmon le saumon fumé
salt le sel
salt water l'eau salée
salty salé(e)
same même
sample l'échantillon *(m)*
sand le sable
sandals les sandales
sandwich le sandwich
  toasted sandwich le croque-
  monsieur
sanitary towel la serviette
  hygiénique
sardine la sardine
satellite dish l'antenne
  parabolique *(f)*
satellite TV la télévision par
  satellite

Saturday samedi
sauce la sauce
  tomato sauce la sauce tomate
saucepan la casserole
saucer la soucoupe
sauerkraut la choucroute
sauna le sauna
sausage la saucisse
to save *(life)* sauver
  (money) épargner ; économiser
saw la scie
to say dire
scales *(for weighing)* la balance
scallop la coquille Saint-Jacques
scarf *(headscarf)* le foulard
  (woollen) l'écharpe *(f)*
scenery le paysage
schedule le programme
school l'école *(f)*
scissors les ciseaux
score *(of match)* le score
to score *(goal, point)* marquer
Scotland l'Écosse *(f)*
Scot *m/f* l' Écossais(e)
Scottish écossais(e)
scouring pad le tampon à récurer
screen *(computer, TV)* l'écran *(m)*
screen wash le lave-glace
screw la vis
screwdriver le tournevis
  phillips screwdriver le tournevis
  cruciforme
scrunchie le chouchou
scuba diving la plongée
  sous-marine
sculpture la sculpture
sea la mer
seafood les fruits de mer
seasickness le mal de mer
seaside le bord de la mer
  at the seaside au bord de la mer
season *(of year)* la saison
  in season de saison
seasonal saisonnier

season ticket la carte
d'abonnement
seat *(chair)* le siège
(in train) la place
(cinema, theatre) le fauteuil
seatbelt la ceinture de sécurité
second second(e)
second *(time)* la seconde
second class seconde classe
second-hand d'occasion
secretary la secrétaire
security guard le/la vigile
sedative le calmant
to see voir
to seize saisir
self-catering flat l'appartement
indépendant (avec cuisine)
self-employed: *to be self*
employed travailler à son compte
self-service le libre-service
to sell vendre
do you sell...? vous vendez...?
sell-by date la date limite de vente
Sellotape® le Scotch®
to send envoyer
senior citizen la personne du
troisième âge
sequel *(book, film)* la suite
serious grave
to serve servir
service *(church)* l'office *(m)*
(in restaurant, shop etc) le service
is service included? le service
est compris?
service charge le service
service station la station-service
set menu le menu à prix fixe
settee le canapé
to sew coudre
sex le sexe
shade l'ombre *(f)*
in the shade à l'ombre
to shake *(bottle, etc)* agiter
shallow peu profond(e)
shampoo le shampooing

shampoo and set le shampooing
et la mise en plis
shandy le panaché
to share partager
shares *(stocks)* les actions
sharp *(razor, knife)* tranchant
to shave se raser
shaving cream la crème à raser
she elle *see* GRAMMAR
sheep le mouton
sheet *(for bed)* le drap
shelf le rayon
shell *(seashell)* le coquillage
shellfish le crustacé
sheltered abrité(e)
sherry le sherry
shine briller
shingles *(illness)* le zona
ship le navire
shirt la chemise
shock absorber l'amortisseur *(m)*
shoe la chaussure
shoelaces les lacets
shoe mender's le cordonnier
shoe polish le cirage
shoeshop le magasin de
chaussures
shop le magasin
to shop faire du shopping
shop assistant le vendeur/la
vendeuse
shop window la vitrine
shopping centre le centre
commercial
shore le rivage
short court(e)
short-sighted myope
shortage le manque
short cut le raccourci
shortly bientôt
shorts le short
shoulder l'épaule *(f)*
to shout crier
show le spectacle

S

to show montrer
shower *(wash)* la douche
  to take a shower prendre une
  douche
shower cap le bonnet de douche
shrimp la crevette grise
to shrink *(clothes)* rétrécir
shut *(closed)* fermé(e)
to shut fermer
shutter *(on window)* le volet
sick *(ill)* malade
  I feel sick j'ai envie de vomir
side dish la garniture
sidelight le feu de position
sidewalk le trottoir
sieve la passoire
sightseeing le tourisme
  to go sightseeing faire du
  tourisme
sightseeing tour l'excursion
  touristique *(f)*
sign *(notice)* le panneau

S

to sign signer
signature la signature
signpost le poteau indicateur
silk la soie
silver l'argent *(m)*
similar (to) semblable (à)
since depuis
to sing chanter
single *(unmarried)* célibataire
  (bed, room) pour une personne
single ticket l'aller simple *(m)*
sink *(washbasin)* l'évier *(m)*
sir Monsieur
sister la sœur
to sit s'asseoir
  sit down! asseyez-vous!
size *(clothes)* la taille
  (shoe) la pointure
skates *(ice)* les patins à glace
  (roller) les patins à roulettes

S

to skate *(on ice)* patiner
  (roller) faire du patin à roulettes
skateboard le skate-board

to go skateboarding faire du
  skate-board
ski le ski
  jet ski le jet-ski
  to go jet skiing faire du jet-ski
to ski faire du ski
ski boots les chaussures de ski
skiing le ski
ski instructor le/la moniteur(-trice)
  de ski
ski jump *(place)* le tremplin de ski
ski lift le remonte-pente
ski pants le fuseau
ski pass le forfait
ski pole le bâton (de ski)
ski run la piste
ski suit la combinaison de ski
skilled adroit(e) ; qualifié(e)
skin la peau
skin diving la plongée sous-marine
skirt la jupe
sky le ciel
slang l'argot *(m)*
slate l'ardoise *(f)*
sledge la luge
to sleep dormir
sleeper *(couchette)* la couchette
  (carriage) la voiture-lit
  (train) le train-couchettes
to sleep in faire la grasse matinée
sleeping bag le sac de couchage
sleeping car la voiture-lit
sleeping pill le somnifère
slice *(bread, cake, etc)* la tranche
  sliced bread le pain en tranches
slide *(photograph)* la diapositive
to slip glisser
slippers les pantoufles
slow lent(e)
to slow down ralentir
slowly lentement
small petit(e)
  smaller than plus petit(e) que
smell l'odeur *(f)*
  a bad smell une mauvaise odeur

smile le sourire
to smile sourire
smoke la fumée
to smoke fumer
  I don't smoke je ne fume pas
smoked fumé(e)
snack le casse-croûte
  to have a snack casser la croûte
snack bar le snack-bar
snail l'escargot *(m)*
snake le serpent
snake bite la morsure de serpent
to sneeze éternuer
snorkel le tuba
snow la neige
to snow: *it's snowing* il neige
snowboard le snowboard
snowboarding le surf des neiges
  to go snowboarding faire du
  snowboard
snow chains les chaînes
snowed up enneigé(e)
snow tyres les pneus cloutés
soap le savon
soap powder *(detergent)* la
  lessive
sober: *to be sober* ne pas avoir bu
socket *(for plug)* la prise de courant
socks les chaussettes
sofa le canapé
sofa bed le canapé-lit
soft doux (douce)
soft drink le soda
software le logiciel
soldier le soldat
sole *(fish)* la sole
  (shoe) la semelle
some de (du/de la/des) *see*
  GRAMMAR
someone quelqu'un
something quelque chose
sometimes quelquefois
son le fils
son-in-law le gendre

song la chanson
soon bientôt
  as soon as possible dès que
  possible
sore douloureux(-euse)
sorry: *I'm sorry!* excusez-moi!
sort la sorte
  what sort de quelle sorte?
sound le bruit
soup le potage ; la soupe
sour aigre
soured cream la crème aigre
south le sud
souvenir le souvenir
spa la station thermale
space la place
spade la pelle
Spain l'Espagne *(f)*
Spanish espagnol(e)
spanner la clé plate
spare parts les pièces de rechange
spare tyre le pneu de rechange
spare wheel la roue de secours
sparkling *(wine)* mousseux(-euse)
  (water) gazeux(-euse)
spark plug la bougie
sparrow le moineau
to speak parler
  do you speak English? vous
  parlez anglais?
special spécial(e)
specialist *(medical)* le/la spécialiste
speciality la spécialité
speeding l'excès de vitesse *(m)*
  a speeding ticket un p.-v. pour
  excès de vitesse
speed limit la limitation de
  vitesse
speedboat le hors-bord
speedometer le compteur
to spell: *how is it spelt?* comment
  ça s'écrit?
spice l'épice *(f)*
spicy épicé(e)
spider l'araignée *(f)*

S

spinach les épinards
spine la colonne vertébrale
spin dryer le sèche-linge
spirits *(alcohol)* les spiritueux
splinter *(in finger)* l'écharde *(f)*
spoke *(of wheel)* le rayon
sponge l'éponge *(f)*
spoon la cuiller
sport le sport
sports shop le magasin de sports
spot *(pimple)* le bouton
sprain l'entorse *(f)*
spring *(season)* le printemps
  (metal) le ressort
spring onion la ciboule
square *(in town)* la place
squash *(game)* le squash
  orange/lemon squash la
  citronnade/l'orangeade *(f)*
squeeze presser
squid le calmar
stadium le stade

S

stage la scène
stain la tache
stained glass window le vitrail
stairs l'escalier *(m)*
stale *(bread)* rassis(e)
stalls *(in theatre)* l'orchestre *(m)*
stamp le timbre
star l'étoile *(f)*
  (celebrity) la vedette
to start commencer
starter *(in meal)* le hors d'œuvre ;
  l'entrée *(f)*
  (in car) le démarreur
station la gare
  bus station la gare routière
  police station le commissariat
  de police
stationer's la papeterie
statue la statue

S

to stay *(remain)* rester
  (reside for while) loger
  I'm staying at... je loge à...
steak le bifteck

to steal voler
steam la vapeur
steel l'acier *(m)*
steep raide
steeple le clocher
steering wheel le volant
step le pas
stepfather le beau-père
stepmother la belle-mère
stereo la chaîne (stéréo)
  personal stereo le baladeur
sterling la livre sterling
stew le ragoût
steward le steward
stewardess l'hôtesse *(f)*
sticking-plaster le sparadrap
still: *still water* l'eau plate *(f)*
sting la piqûre
to sting piquer
stitches *(surgical)* les points de
  suture
stock cube le bouillon-Kub®
stockings les bas
stomach l'estomac *(m)*
stomachache: *to have a
  stomachache* avoir mal au ventre
stomach upset l'estomac dérangé
stone la pierre
to stop arrêter
store *(shop)* le magasin
storey l'étage *(m)*
storm l'orage *(m)*
story l'histoire *(f)*
straightaway tout de suite
straight on tout droit
straw *(for drinking)* la paille
strawberry la fraise
stream le ruisseau
street la rue
street map le plan des rues
strength la force
stress le stress
strike *(of workers)* la grève
string la ficelle

striped rayé(e)
stroke *(haemorrhage)* l'attaque (d'apoplexie)
  to have a stroke avoir une attaque
strong fort(e)
stuck bloqué(e)
student *(male)* l'étudiant *(female)* l'étudiante
student concession le tarif étudiant
stuffed farci(e)
stupid stupide
subscription l'abonnement *(m)*
subtitles les sous-titres
to succeed réussir
suddenly soudain
suede le daim
sugar le sucre
  icing sugar le sucre glace
sugar-free sans sucre
suit *(man's)* le costume *(woman's)* le tailleur
suitcase la valise
sum la somme
summer l'été *(m)*
summer holidays les vacances d'été
sun le soleil
sunbathe prendre un bain de soleil
sunblock l'écran total *(m)*
sunburn le coup de soleil
Sunday le dimanche
sunflower le tournesol
sunglasses les lunettes de soleil
sunny: *it's sunny* il fait beau
sunrise le lever du soleil
sunroof le toit ouvrant
sunscreen *(lotion)* l'écran solaire *(m)*
sunset le coucher du soleil
sunshade le parasol
sunstroke l'insolation *(f)*
suntan lotion le lait solaire
supermarket le supermarché

supper *(dinner)* le souper
supplement le supplément
to supply fournir
surf le surf
to surf faire du surf
surfboard la planche de surf
surfing le surf
surgery *(operation)* l'opération chirurgicale *(f)*
surname le nom de famille
surprise la surprise
swallow *(bird)* l'hirondelle *(f)*
to swallow avaler
swan le cygne
to sweat transpirer
sweater le pull
sweatshirt le sweat-shirt
sweet sucré(e)
sweetener l'édulcorant *(m)*
sweets les bonbons
to swell *(bump, eye, etc)* enfler
to swim nager
swimming pool la piscine
swimsuit le maillot de bain
swing *(for children)* la balançoire
Swiss suisse
switch le bouton
to switch off éteindre
to switch on allumer
Switzerland la Suisse
swollen enflé(e)
synagogue la synagogue
syringe la seringue

T

table la table
tablecloth la nappe
table tennis le ping-pong
table wine le vin de tablee
tablet le comprimé
to take *(something)* prendre
to take away *(something)* emporter

t

to take off *(clothes)* enlever
talc le talc
to talk (to) parler (à)
tall grand(e)
tampons les tampons hygiéniques
tan le bronzage
tangerine la mandarine
tank *(petrol)* le réservoir
  (fish) l'aquarium *(m)*
tap le robinet
tape le ruban
  (cassette) la cassette
  adhesive tape le Scotch®
  video tape la cassette vidéo
tape measure le mètre à ruban
tape recorder le magnétophone
tarragon l'estragon *(m)*
tart la tarte
tartar sauce la sauce tartare
taste le goût
to taste goûter
  can I taste some? je peux goûter?
tax l'impôt *(m)*
taxi le taxi
taxi rank la station de taxis
tea le thé
  herbal tea la tisane
  lemon tea le thé au citron
  tea with milk le thé au lait
teabag le sachet de thé
teapot la théière
teaspoon la cuiller à café
tea towel le torchon
to teach enseigner
teacher le professeur
tear *(in material)* la déchirure
teenager l'adolescent(e)
teeth les dents
telegram le télégramme
telephone le téléphone
  mobile telephone le (téléphone) portable
to telephone téléphoner

telephone box la cabine téléphonique
telephone call le coup de téléphone
telephone card la télécarte
telephone directory l'annuaire *(m)*
telephone number le numéro de téléphone
television la télévision
telex le télex
to tell dire
temperature la température
  to have a temperature avoir de la fièvre
temporary temporaire
ten dix
tendon le tendon
tennis le tennis
tennis ball la balle de tennis
tennis court le court de tennis
tennis racket la raquette de tennis
tent la tente
tent peg le piquet de tente
terminal *(airport)* l'aérogare *(f)*
terrace la terrasse
terrorists les terroristes
testicles les testicules
to thank remercier
thank you merci
  thank you very much merci beaucoup
that cela
  that one celui-là/celle-là
the le/la/l'/les see **GRAMMAR**
theatre le théâtre
theft le vol
their *(sing)* leur
  (plural) leurs see **GRAMMAR**
them eux
there là
there is/are... il y a...
thermometer le thermomètre
these ces
  these ones ceux-ci/celles-ci
they ils/elles see **GRAMMAR**

thick *(not thin)* épais(se)

thief le voleur/la voleuse

thin *(person)* mince

thing la chose
  my things mes affaires

to think penser

third troisième

thirsty: *I'm thirsty* j'ai soif

this ceci
  this one celui-ci/celle-ci

thorn l'épine *(f)*

those ces
  those ones ceux-là/celles-là

thousand mille

thread le fil

throat la gorge

throat lozenges les pastilles pour la gorge

through à travers

thrush *(candida)* le muguet

thumb le pouce

thunder le tonnerre

thunderstorm l'orage *(m)*

Thursday le jeudi

thyme le thym

ticket *(bus, tube, cinema, museum)* le ticket
  (plane, train, theatre, concert) le billet
  a single ticket un aller simple
  a return ticket un (billet) aller retour
  book of tickets le carnet de tickets

ticket inspector le contrôleur/la contrôleuse

ticket office le guichet

tide la marée
  low tide la marée basse
  high tide la marée haute

tie la cravate
  bow tie le nœud papillon

tight *(fitting)* serré(e)

tights le collant

tile *(on roof)* la tuile
  (on wall, floor) le carreau

till *(cash desk)* la caisse

till *(until)* jusqu'à
  till 2 o'clock jusqu'à deux heures

time le temps
  (of day) l'heure *(f)*
  this time cette fois
  what time is it? quelle heure est-il?

timer le minuteur

timetable l'horaire *(m)*

tin *(can)* la boîte

tinfoil le papier d'alu(minium)

tin-opener l'ouvre-boîtes *(m)*

tiny minuscule

tip *(to waiter, etc)* le pourboire

to tip *(waiter, etc)* donner un pourboire à

tipped *(cigarette)* à bout filtre

Tipp-Ex® le Tipp-Ex®

tired fatigué(e)

tissue *(Kleenex®)* le kleenex®

to à
  (with name of country) en/au
  to London à Londres
  to the airport à l'aéroport
  to France en France
  to Canada au Canada

toad le crapaud

toadstool le champignon vénéneux

toast *(to eat)* le pain grillé ; le toast

tobacco le tabac

tobacconist's le bureau de tabac

today aujourd'hui

toddler le bambin

toe le doigt de pied

together ensemble

toilet les toilettes
  toilet for disabled les toilettes pour handicapés

toilet brush la balayette pour les WC

toilet paper le papier hygiénique

toiletries les articles de toilette

token le jeton

139

t

toll (motorway) le péage
tomato la tomate
  tomato soup la soupe de tomates
  tinned tomatoes les tomates en boîte
tomorrow demain
  tomorrow morning demain matin
  tomorrow afternoon demain après-midi
  tomorrow evening demain soir
tongue la langue
tonic water le tonic
tonight ce soir
tonsillitis l'angine *(f)*
too (also) aussi
  it's too big c'est trop grand
  it's too hot (weather, room) il fait trop chaud
  too noisy il y a trop de bruit
toolkit la trousse à outils
tools les outils
tooth la dent
toothache le mal de dents
  I have toothache j'ai mal aux dents
toothbrush la brosse à dents
toothpaste le dentifrice
top: *the top floor* le dernier étage
top (of jar, bottle) le bouchon
  (of pen) le capuchon
  (of pyjamas, bikini, etc) le haut
  (of hill, mountain) le sommet
  on top of sur
topless: *to go topless* enlever le haut
torch la lampe de poche
torn déchiré(e)
total (amount) le total
to touch toucher
tough (meat) dur(e)
tour l'excursion *(f)*
  guided tour la visite guidée
tour guide le/la guide

tour operator le tour-opérateur ; le voyagiste
tourist le/la touriste
tourist office le syndicat d'initiative
tourist route l'itinéraire touristique *(m)*
tourist ticket le billet touristique
to tow remorquer
towbar (on car) le crochet d'attelage
tow rope le câble de remorquage
towel la serviette
tower la tour
town la ville
town centre le centre-ville
town hall la mairie
town plan le plan de la ville
toy le jouet
toyshop le magasin de jouets
tracksuit le survêtement
traditional traditionnel(-elle)
traffic la circulation
traffic jam l'embouteillage *(m)*
traffic lights les feux
trailer la remorque
train le train
  by train par le train
  the next train le prochain train
  the first train le premier train
  the last train le dernier train
trainers les baskets
tram le tramway
tranquilliser le tranquillisant
to translate traduire
translation la traduction
to travel voyager
travel agent's l'agence de voyages *(f)*
travel guide le guide
travel pass la carte de transport
travel sickness le mal des transports
traveller's cheques les chèques de voyage

tray le plateau
tree l'arbre *(m)*
trip l'excursion *(f)*
trolley le chariot
trouble les ennuis
trousers le pantalon
trout la truite
truck le camion
true vrai(e)
trunk *(luggage)* la malle
trunks *(swimming)* le maillot (de bain)
to try essayer
to try on *(clothes, shoes)* essayer
t-shirt le tee-shirt
Tuesday le mardi
tulip la tulipe
tumble dryer le sèche-linge
tuna le thon
tunnel le tunnel
turkey la dinde
to turn tourner
  to turn round faire demi-tour
to turn off *(light, etc)* éteindre
  (to turn off engine) couper le moteur
to turn on *(light, etc)* allumer
  (engine) mettre en marche
turnip le navet
turquoise *(colour)* turquoise
tweezers la pince à épiler
twice deux fois
twin-bedded room la chambre à deux lits
twins *(male)* les jumeaux
  (female) les jumelles
  identical twins les vrais jumeaux
two deux
to type taper à la machine
typical typique
tyre le pneu
tyre pressure la pression des pneus

U

ugly laid(e)
ulcer l'ulcère *(m)*
  mouth ulcer l'aphte *(m)*
umbrella le parapluie
  (sunshade) le parasol
uncle l'oncle *(m)*
uncomfortable inconfortable
unconscious sans connaissance
under sous
undercooked pas assez cuit(e)
underground le métro
underpants *(man's)* le caleçon
underpass le passage souterrain
to understand comprendre
  I don't understand je ne comprends pas
  do you understand? vous comprenez?
underwear les sous-vêtements
to undress se déshabiller
unemployed au chômage
to unfasten *(clothes, etc)* défaire
  (door) ouvrir
United Kingdom le Royaume-Uni
United States les États Unis
university l'université *(f)*
unkind pas gentil(-ille)
unleaded petrol l'essence sans plomb *(f)*
to unpack *(suitcase)* défaire
unpleasant désagréable
to unscrew dévisser
to get up *(out of bed)* se lever
upstairs en haut
urgent urgent(e)
urine l'urine *(f)*
us nous *see* GRAMMAR
to use utiliser
useful utile
usual habituel(-elle)
usually d'habitude
U-turn le demi-tour

V

vacancy (in hotel) la chambre
vaccination le vaccin
vacuum cleaner l'aspirateur (m)
vagina le vagin
valid (ticket, driving licence, etc) valable
valley la vallée
valuable d'une grande valeur
valuables les objets de valeur
value la valeur
valve la soupape
van la camionnette
vanilla la vanille
vase le vase
VAT la TVA
veal le veau
vegan végétalien(ne)
vegetables les légumes
vegetarian végétarien(ne)
 I'm a vegetarian je suis végétarien(ne)
vehicle le véhicule
vein la veine
Velcro® le Velcro®
velvet le velours
vending machine le distributeur automatique
venereal disease la maladie vénérienne
venison le chevreuil
ventilator le ventilateur
vermouth le vermouth
very très
vest le maillot de corps
vet le/la vétérinaire
via par
to video (from TV) enregistrer
video (machine) le magnétoscope
 (cassette) la (cassette) vidéo
video camera la caméra vidéo
video game le jeu vidéo
video recorder le magnétoscope

video shop le vidéoclub
view la vue
 a room with a sea view une chambre avec vue sur la mer
villa la maison de campagne
village le village
vinaigrette la vinaigrette
vinegar le vinaigre
vineyard le vignoble
violet la violette
viper la vipère
visa le visa
visit le séjour
 visit to France le séjour en France
to visit visiter
visiting hours les heures de visite
visitor le/la visiteur(-euse)
vitamin la vitamine
vodka la vodka
volcano le volcan
volleyball le volley-ball
voltage le voltage
to vomit vomir
voucher le bon

W

wage le salaire
waist la taille
waistcoat le gilet
to wait for attendre
waiter le/la serveur(-euse)
waiting room la salle d'attente
waitress la serveuse
to wake up se réveiller
Wales le pays de Galles
walk la promenade
 to go for a walk faire une promenade
to walk aller à pied ; marcher
walking boots les chaussures de marche
walking stick la canne

Walkman® le walkman®
wall le mur
wallet le portefeuille
walnut la noix
to want vouloir *see* **GRAMMAR**
  I want... je veux...
  we want... nous voulons...
war la guerre
ward *(hospital)* la salle
wardrobe l'armoire *(f)*
warehouse l'entrepôt *(m)*
warm chaud(e)
  it's warm (weather) il fait bon
  it's too warm il fait trop chaud
to warm up *(milk, etc)* faire chauffer
warning triangle le triangle de présignalisation
to wash laver
  to wash oneself se laver
washbasin le lavabo
washing machine la machine à laver
washing powder la lessive
washing-up bowl la cuvette
washing-up liquid le produit pour la vaisselle
wasp la guêpe
waste bin la poubelle
watch la montre
to watch *(look at)* regarder
watchstrap le bracelet de montre
water l'eau *(f)*
  bottled water l'eau en bouteille
  cold water l'eau froide
  drinking water (fit to drink) l'eau potable
  hot water l'eau chaude
  sparkling mineral water l'eau minérale gazeuse
  still mineral water l'eau minérale plate
waterfall la cascade
water heater le chauffe-eau
watermelon la pastèque
waterproof imperméable
water-skiing le ski nautique

water sports les sports nautiques
waterwings les bracelets gonflables
waves *(on sea)* les vagues
waxing *(hair removal)* l'épilation à la cire *(f)*
way *(manner)* la manière
  (route) le chemin
way in *(entrance)* l'entrée *(f)*
way out *(exit)* la sortie
we nous *see* **GRAMMAR**
weak faible
  (coffee, etc) léger(-ère)
to wear porter
weather le temps
weather forecast la météo
web *(spider)* la toile d'araignée
website le site web
wedding le mariage
wedding anniversary l'anniversaire de mariage *(m)*
wedding dress la robe de mariée
wedding present le cadeau de mariage
Wednesday le mercredi
week la semaine
  last week la semaine dernière
  next week la semaine prochaine
  per week par semaine
  this week cette semaine
  during the week pendant la semaine ; en semaine
weekday le jour de semaine
weekend le week-end
  next weekend le week-end prochain
  this weekend ce week-end
weekly par semaine ; hebdomadaire
  (pass, ticket) valable pendant une semaine
to weigh peser
weight le poids
welcome! bienvenu(e)!

W

W

well *(for water)* le puits
well *(healthy)* en bonne santé
  I'm very well je vais très bien
  he's not well il est souffrant
well done *(steak)* bien cuit(e)
wellingtons les bottes en
  caoutchouc
Welsh gallois(e)
west l'ouest *(m)*
wet mouillé(e)
wetsuit la combinaison de plongée
what que ; quel/quelle ; quoi
  what is it? qu'est-ce que c'est?
wheel la roue
wheelchair le fauteuil roulant
wheel clamp le sabot de Denver
when quand
  (at what time?) à quelle heure?
  when is it? c'est quand? ; à
  quelle heure?
where où
  where is it? c'est où?
  where is the hotel? où est
  l'hôtel?
which quel/quelle
  which (one)? lequel/laquelle?
  which (ones)?
  lesquels/lesquelles?
while pendant que
  in a while bientôt ; tout à l'heure
whipped cream la crème fouettée
whisky le whisky
white blanc (blanche)
who qui
  who is it? qui c'est?
whole entier(-ière)
wholemeal bread le pain complet
whose: *whose is it?* c'est à qui?
why pourquoi
wide large
widow la veuve
widower le veuf
width la largeur
wife la femme
wig la perruque

wildlife la nature
to win gagner
wind le vent
windbreak *(camping etc)* le
  pare-vent
windmill le moulin à vent
window la fenêtre
  (shop) la vitrine
windscreen le pare-brise
windscreen wipers les essuie-
  glaces
windsurfing la planche à voile
to go windsurfing faire de la
  planche à voile
windy: *it's windy* il y a du vent
wine le vin
  dry wine le vin sec
  house wine le vin en pichet
  red wine le vin rouge
  rosé wine le rosé
  sparkling wine le vin mousseux
  sweet wine le vin doux
  white wine le vin blanc
wine list la carte des vins
wing *(bird, aircraft)* l'aile *(f)*
wing mirror le rétroviseur latéral
winter l'hiver *(m)*
with avec
  with ice avec des glaçons
  with milk avec du lait
  with sugar avec du sucre
without sans
  without ice sans glaçons
  without milk sans lait
  without sugar sans sucre
wolf le loup
woman la femme
wonderful merveilleux(-euse)
wood le bois
wooden en bois
wool la laine
word le mot
work le travail
to work *(person)* travailler
  (machine, car) fonctionner ;
  marcher

it doesn't work ça ne marche pas
 to work from home travailler à
 la maison
world le monde
worried inquiet(-iète)
worse pire
worth: it's worth... ça vaut...
to wrap (up) emballer
wrapping paper le papier
 d'emballage
wrinkles les rides
wrist le poignet
to write écrire
 please write it down vous me
 l'écrivez, s'il vous plaît?
writing paper le papier à lettres
wrong faux (fausse)

X

X-ray la radiographie

Y

yacht le yacht
year l'an (m) ; l'année (f)
 this year cette année
 next year l'année prochaine
 last year l'année dernière
yellow jaune
Yellow Pages les pages jaunes

yes oui
 yes please oui, merci
yesterday hier
yet: not yet pas encore
yoghurt le yaourt
 plain yoghurt le yaourt nature
yolk le jaune d'œuf
you (familiar) tu
 (polite) vous see **GRAMMAR**
young jeune
your (familiar sing) ton/ta
 (familiar pl) tes
 (polite sing) votre
 (polite pl) vos see **GRAMMAR**
 your passport ton passeport
 your room ta chambre
 your suitcases tes valises
 your passport votre passeport
 your room votre chambre
 your suitcases vos valises
youth hostel l'auberge de
 jeunesse (f)

Z

zebra crossing le passage pour
 piétons
zero le zéro
zip la fermeture éclair
zone la zone
zoo le zoo

à to ; at
abbaye f abbey
abcès m abscess
abeille f bee
abîmer to damage
abonné(e) m/f subscriber ;
  season ticket holder
abonnement m subscription ;
  season ticket
aboyer to bark
abri m shelter
abrité(e) sheltered
accélérateur m accelerator
accepter to accept
accès m access

  ACCÈS AUX TRAINS
  to the trains

  accès aux quais to the trains
  accès interdit no entry
  accès réservé authorized entry
  only
accident m accident
accompagner to accompany
accord m agreement
accotement m verge
accueil m reception
accueillir to greet ; to welcome
ACF m Automobile Club de France
achat m purchase
acheter to buy
acier m steel
acte de naissance m birth
  certificate
actions fpl shares (stocks)
activité f activity
adaptateur m adaptor (electrical)
addition f bill
adhérent(e) m/f member
adolescent(e) m/f teenager
adresse f address
adresse électronique e-mail
  address
adresser to address
  adressez-vous à enquire at (office)
adroit(e) skilful

adulte m/f adult
aérogare f terminal
aéroglisseur m hovercraft
aéroport m airport
affaires fpl business ; belongings
  bonnes affaires bargain
affiche f poster ; notice
affreux(-euse) awful
âge m age
  d'un certain âge middle-aged
  du troisième âge senior citizen
âgé(e) elderly
  âgé de aged
agence f agency ; branch
  agence de voyages travel agency
  agence immobilière estate
  agent's
agenda m diary
  agenda électronique m personal
  organizer (electronic)
agent m agent
  agent de police policeman
agiter to shake

  AGITER AVANT EMPLOI
  shake before use

agneau m lamb
agrandissement m enlargement
agréable pleasant ; nice
agréé(e) registered ; authorized
agression f attack (mugging)
aider to help
aigre sour
aiguille f needle
ail m garlic
aimant m magnet
aimer to enjoy ; to love (person)
air: en plein air in the open air
aire: aire de jeux play area
  aire de repos rest area
  aire de service service area
  aire de stationnement layby
airelles fpl bilberries ; cranberries
alarme f alarm
alcool m alcohol ; fruit brandy
alcoolisé(e) alcoholic
alentours mpl outskirts
algues fpl seaweed
alimentation f food

a

allée f driveway ; path
allégé(e) low- fat
Allemagne f Germany
allemand(e) German
aller to go
aller (simple) m single ticket
aller-retour m return ticket
allergie f allergy
allô? hello (on telephone)
allumage m ignition
allumé(e) on (light)
allume-feu m fire lighter
allumer to turn on ; to light
  allumez vos phares switch on
  headlights
allumette f match
Alpes Alps
alpinisme m mountaineering
alsacien(ne) Alsatian
ambassade f embassy
ambulance f ambulance
améliorer to improve
amende f fine
amer(-ère) bitter
américain(e) American
Amérique f America
ameublé(e) furnished
ami(e) m/f friend
  petit(e) ami(e),
  boyfriend/girlfriend
amortisseur m shock absorber
amour m love
  faire l'amour to make love
ampoule f blister ; light bulb
amusant(e) funny (amusing)
amuser to entertain
  s'amuser (bien) to enjoy oneself
an m year
  Nouvel An m New Year
analgésique m painkiller
ananas m pineapple
ancien(ne) old ; former
ancre f anchor
anesthésique m anaesthetic
ange m angel
angine f tonsillitis
  angine de poitrine angina
anglais m English (language)
anglais(e) English

Angleterre f England
animal m animal
  animal de compagnie pet
animation f entertainment ; activity
anis m aniseed
anisette f aniseed liqueur
année f year ; vintage
  bonne année! happy New Year!
anniversaire m anniversary ;
  birthday
annonce f advertisement
annuaire m directory
annulation f cancellation
annuler to cancel
antenne f aerial
  antenne parabolique f satellite
  dish
anti-insecte m insect repellent
antibiotique m antibiotic
antigel m antifreeze
antihistaminique m antihistamine
antimoustique m mosquito
  repellent
antiquaire m/f antique dealer
antiquités mpl antiques
antiseptique m antiseptic
antivol m bike lock
AOC abbrev. of appellation
  d'origine contrôlée

AOÛT August

apéritif m apéritif
aphte m mouth ulcer
appareil m appliance ; camera
  appareil acoustique hearing aid
  appareil photo camera
appartement m apartment ; flat
appât m bait (for fishing)
appel m phone call
appeler to call (speak, phone)
  appeler en PCV to reverse the
  charges
appendicite f appendicitis
apporter to bring
apprendre to learn

APPUYER press

après after
après-midi m afternoon

148

après-rasage m after-shave
après-shampooing m conditioner
aquarium m fish tank
arachide f groundnut
araignée f spider
arbitre m referee
arbre m tree
arc-en-ciel m rainbow
ardoise f slate
arête f fishbone
argent m money ; silver (metal)
  argent de poche pocket money
  argent liquide cash
argot m slang
armoire f wardrobe
arranger to arrange

ARRÊT stop

  arrêt d'autobus bus stop
  arrêt facultatif request stop
arrêter to arrest ; to stop
  arrêter le moteur turn off engine
arrêtez stop
arrhes fpl deposit (part payment)
arrière m rear ; back

ARRIVÉES arrivals

arriver to arrive; to happen
arrondissement m district (in Paris)
art m art
arthrite f arthritis
article m item ; article
  articles de toilette toiletries
articulation f joint (body)
artificiel artificial
artisan(e) craftsman/woman
artisanat m arts and crafts
artiste m/f artist

ASCENSEUR lift

aspirateur m vacuum cleaner
aspirine f aspirin
assaisonnement m seasoning ; dressing
asseoir to sit (someone) down
  s'asseoir to sit down
assez enough ; quite (rather)
assiette f plate
associé(e) m/f partner (business)

assorti(e) assorted ; matching
assurance f insurance
assuré(e) insured
assurer to assure ; to insure
asthme m asthma
atelier m workshop ; artist's studio
attacher to fasten (seatbelt)
attaque f fit (medical)
  attaque (d'apoplexie) stroke
attendre to wait (for)
attention! look out!
  attention au feu danger of fire
  faire attention to be careful
atterrissage m landing (aircraft)
attestation f certificate
attrayant(e) attractive
au-delà de beyond
au-dessus de above; on top of
au lieu de instead of
au revoir goodbye
au secours! help!
aube f dawn
auberge f inn
  auberge de jeunesse youth hostel
aubergine f aubergine
aucun(e) none ; no ; not any
audiophone m hearing aid
augmenter to increase
aujourd'hui today
aussi also
aussitôt immediately
  aussitôt que possible as soon as possible
Australie f Australia
australien(ne) Australian
autel m altar
auteur m author
authentique genuine
auto-école f driving school
auto-stop m hitchhiking
autobus m bus
autocar m coach
automatique automatic
automne m autumn
automobiliste m/f motorist
autoradio m car radio
autorisé(e) permitted ; authorized
autoroute f motorway

a

autre other
  autres directions other routes
avalanche f avalanche
avaler to swallow
  ne pas avaler not to be taken
  internally
avance f advance
  à l'avance in advance
avant before ; front
  à l'avant at the front
  en avant forward
avec with
avenir m future
avenue f avenue
avertir to inform ; to warn
aveugle blind
avion m aeroplane
aviron m oar ; rowing (sport)
avis m notice ; warning
aviser to advise
avocat m avocado ; lawyer
avoine f oats
avoir to have see GRAMMAR
avortement m abortion

a

AVRIL April

axe m axle (car)

B

bacon m bacon
bagages mpl luggage
  bagages à main hand luggage
  faire les bagages to pack
bague f ring (on finger)
baguette f stick of French bread
baie f bay (along coast)
baignade f bathing

BAIGNADE INTERDITE no bathing

bain m bath
  bain moussant bubble bath
baiser kiss
baisser to lower
bal m ball ; dance
balai m broom (brush)
  balai à laver mop (for floor)
balance f scales (for weighing)
balançoire f swing (for children)

b

balcon m circle (theatre) ; balcony
ball-trap m clay pigeon shooting
balle f ball (small: golf, tennis, etc)
ballet m ballet
ballon m balloon ; ball (large) ;
  brandy glass
bambin m toddler
banane f banana ; bumbag
banc m seat ; bench
banlieue f suburbs
banque f bank
baptême m christening
bar m bar
  bar à café unlicensed bar (Switz.)
barbe f beard
barbecue m barbecue
barque f rowing boat
barrage m dam
  barrage routier road block
barré: route barrée road closed
barrer to cross out
barrière f barrier
bas m bottom (of page, etc) ;
  stocking
  en bas below ; downstairs
bas(se) low
baskets fpl trainers
bassin m pond ; washing-up bowl
bateau m boat ; ship
  bateau à rames rowing boat
  bateau-mouche river boat
bâtiment m building
bâton (de ski) m ski pole
batte f bat (baseball, cricket)
batterie f battery (for car)
  batterie à plat flat battery
baume pour les lèvres m lip salve
bavoir m bib (baby's)
beau (belle) lovely ; handsome ;
  beautiful ; nice (enjoyable)
beau-frère m brother-in-law
beau-père m father-in-law ; stepfather
beaucoup (de) much/many ; a lot
  of
bébé m baby
beignet m fritter ; doughnut
belge Belgian
Belgique f Belgium

belle-fille f daughter-in-law
belle-mère f mother-in-law ; step-mother
béquilles fpl crutches
berger m shepherd
berlingots mpl boiled sweets
besoin: avoir besoin de to need
beurre m butter
  beurre doux unsalted butter
biberon m baby's bottle
bibliothèque f library
bicyclette f bicycle
bien well ; right ; good
  bien cuit(e) well done (steak)
bientôt soon ; shortly
bienvenu(e) welcome!
bière f beer
  bière (à la) pression draught beer
  bière blonde lager
  bière bouteille bottled lager
  bière brune bitter
bifteck m steak
bijouterie f jeweller's ; jewellery
bijoux mpl jewellery
bikini m bikini
billet m note ; ticket
  billet aller-retour return ticket
  billet d'avion plane ticket
  billet de banque banknote
  billet simple one-way ticket

  BILLETS tickets

biologique organic
biscotte f breakfast biscuit ; rusk
biscuit m biscuit
bisque f thick seafood soup
blanc (blanche) white ; blank
  en blanc blank (on form)
blanc d'œuf m egg white
blanchisserie f laundry
blé m wheat
blessé(e) injured
blesser to injure
bleu m bruise
bleu(e) blue ; very rare (steak)
  bleu marine navy blue
bloc-notes m note pad
blond(e) fair (hair)
bloqué(e) stuck

body m body (clothing)
bœuf m beef
boire to drink
bois m wood
boisson f drink
  boisson non alcoolisée soft drink
boîte f can ; box
  boîte à fusibles fuse box
  boîte à lettres post box
  boîte de nuit night club
  boîte de vitesses gearbox
bol m bowl (for soup, etc)
bombe f aerosol ; bomb
bon m token ; voucher
bon (bonne) good ; right ; nice
  bon anniversaire happy birthday
  bon marché inexpensive
bonbon m sweet
bondé(e) crowded
bonhomme m chap
  bonhomme de neige snowman
bonjour hello ; good morning/afternoon
bonnet m bonnet ; hat
  bonnet de bain bathing cap
bonneterie f hosiery
bonsoir good evening
bord m border ; edge ; verge
  à bord on board
  au bord de la mer at the seaside
bosse f lump (swelling)
botte f boot ; bunch
bottillons mpl ankle boots
bouche f mouth
  bouche d'incendie fire hydrant
bouché(e) blocked
bouchée f mouthful ; chocolate
boucherie f butcher's shop
bouchon m cork ; plug (for sink) ; top (of jar, bottle)
boucle d'oreille f earring
boue f mud
bouée de sauvetage f life belt
bougie f candle; spark plug
bouillabaisse f rich fish soup/stew
bouilli(e) boiled
bouillir to boil
bouilloire f kettle
bouillon m stock

b

bouillotte f hot-water bottle
boulangerie f bakery
boule f ball
boules fpl game similar to bowls
bouquet m bunch (of flowers)
Bourse f stock exchange
boussole f compass
bout m end
  à bout filtre filter-tipped
bouteille f bottle
boutique f shop
bouton m button ; switch ; spot
  bouton d'or buttercup
  bouton de fièvre cold sore
  boutons de manchette cufflinks
boxe f boxing
boxer-short m boxer shorts
bracelet m bracelet
  bracelet de montre watchstrap
braisé(e) braised
bras m arm
brasserie f café ; brewery
Bretagne f Brittany
breton(ne) from Brittany
bricolage m do-it-yourself
briller to shine
brioche f brioche
briquet m cigarette lighter
briser to break ; to smash
britannique British
brocante f second-hand goods ;
  flea market
broche f brooch ; spit
brochette f skewer ; kebab
brocoli m broccoli
brodé main hand-embroidered
bronzage m suntan
bronze bronze
brosse f brush
  brosse à cheveux hairbrush
  brosse à dents toothbrush
brouillard m fog
bru f daughter-in-law
bruit m noise
brûlé(e) burnt
brûler to burn
brûlures d'estomac fpl heartburn
brumeux(-euse) misty
brun(e) brown ; dark

brushing m blow-dry
brut(e) gross ; raw
Bruxelles Brussels
bûche f log (for fire)
buisson m bush
bulletin de consigne m left-
  luggage ticket
bureau m desk ; office
  bureau de change foreign
  exchange office
  bureau de location booking
  office
  bureau de poste post office
  bureau de renseignements
  information office
  bureau des objets trouvés lost
  property office
bus m bus
butane m camping gas

C

ça va it's OK
cabaret m cabaret
cabine f beach hut ; cubicle ; cabin
  cabine d'essayage changing
  room
cabinet m office
câble de remorque m tow rope
cacahuète f peanut
cacao m cocoa
cacher to hide
cadeau m gift
cadenas m padlock
cadre m picture frame
cafard m cockroach
café m coffee ; café
  café au lait white coffee
  café crème white coffee
  café décaféiné decaff coffee
  café instantané instant coffee
  café noir black coffee
cafetière f coffee pot
cahier m exercise book

CAISSE cash desk

caisse f cash desk ; case
  caisse d'épargne savings bank
caissier(ière) m/f cashier ; teller

152

calculatrice f calculator
caleçon m boxer shorts
calendrier m calendar ; timetable
calmant m sedative
cambriolage m break-in
cambrioleur(-euse) m/f burglar
caméra vidéo f video camera
caméscope m camcorder
camion m lorry ; truck
camionnette f van
camomille f camomile
campagne f countryside ; campaign
camper to camp
camping m camping ; camp-site
  camping sauvage camping on unofficial sites
  camping-gaz camping stove
Canada m Canada
canadien(ne) Canadian
canal m canal
canapé m sofa ; open sandwich
  canapé-lit sofa bed
canard m duck
canif m penknife
canne f walking stick
  canne à pêche fishing rod
cannelle f cinnamon
canoë m canoe
canot m boat
  canot de sauvetage lifeboat
canotage m boating
canton m state (Switz.)
caoutchouc m rubber (material)
capable efficient (person)
capitale f capital (city)
capot m bonnet ; hood (of car)
câpres fpl capers
capuchon m hood ; top (of pen)
car m coach
carabine de chasse f hunting rifle
carafe f carafe ; decanter
caravane f caravan
carburateur m carburettor
Carême m Lent
carnet m notebook ; book
  carnet de billets book of tickets
  carnet de chèques cheque book
carotte f carrot
carré m square

carreau m tile (on wall, floor)
carrefour m crossroads
carte f map ; card ; menu ; pass (bus, train)
  carte bleue credit card
  carte d'abonnement season ticket
  carte d'embarquement boarding card/pass
  carte d'identité identity card
  carte de crédit credit card
  carte des vins wine list
  carte du jour menu of the day
  carte grise log book (car)
  carte orange monthly or yearly season ticket
  carte postale postcard
  carte routière road map
  carte vermeille senior citizen's rail pass
  carte verte green card
cartes (à jouer) fpl playing cards
carton m cardboard
cartouche f carton (of cigarettes)
cas m case
cascade f waterfall
case postale f PO Box (Switz.)
caserne f barracks
casier m rack ; locker
casino m casino
casque m helmet
  casque (à écouteurs) headphones
  casque protecteur crash helmet
casquette f cap (hat)
cassé(e) broken

CASSE-CROÛTE snacks

casser to break
  casser la croûte to have a snack
casserole f saucepan
cassette f cassette
catch m wrestling
cathédrale f cathedral
catholique Catholic
cause f cause
  pour cause de on account of
caution f security (for loan) ; deposit
  caution à verser deposit required
cave f cellar

C

caveau m cellar
caviar m caviar(e)
CD m CD
ceci this

CÉDEZ LE PASSAGE give way

CE f EC
ceinture f belt
  ceinture de sécurité seatbelt
  ceinture porte-monnaie money-belt
cela that
célèbre famous
célibataire single (unmarried)
cendrier m ashtray
cent m hundred
centimètre m centimetre
central(e) central
centre m centre
  centre commercial shopping centre
  centre de loisirs leisure centre
  centre équestre riding school
  centre ville city centre
céramique f ceramics
cercle m circle ; ring
céréales fpl cereal (for breakfast)
cerise f cherry
certain(e) certain (sure)
certificat m certificate
cerveau m brain
cervelle f brains (as food)
cesser to stop
cette this ; that
ceux-ci/celles-ci these ones
ceux-là/celles-là those ones
CFF mpl Swiss Railways
chacun/chacune each
chaîne f chain ; channel ; (mountain) range
  chaîne (stéréo) stereo
  chaînes snow chains
  chaînes obligatoires snow chains compulsory
chair f flesh
chaise f chair
  chaise longue deckchair
châle m shawl
chalet m chalet

chambre f bedroom ; room
  chambre à air inner tube
  chambre à coucher bedroom
  chambre à deux lits twin-bedded room
  chambre d'hôte bed and breakfast
  chambre individuelle single room
  chambre pour deux personnes double room

CHAMBRES rooms to let

champ m field
  champ de courses racecourse
champagne m champagne
champignon m mushroom
  champignon vénéneux toadstool
chance f luck
change m exchange
changement m change
changer to change
  changer de l'argent to change money
  changer de train to change train
  se changer to change clothes
chanson f song
chanter to sing
chanterelle f chanterelle
chantier m building site ; roadworks
chapeau m hat
chapelle f chapel
chaque each ; every
charbon m coal
  charbon de bois charcoal
charcuterie f pork butcher's ; delicatessen ; cooked meat
chariot m trolley
charter m charter flight
chasse f hunting ; shooting
  chasse gardée private hunting
  chasse-neige m snowplough
chasser to hunt
chasseur m hunter
chat m cat
châtaigne f chestnut
château m castle ; mansion

CHAUD hot

154

chauffage m heating
chauffer to heat up *(milk, water)*
chauffeur m driver
chaussée f carriageway
  chaussée déformée uneven road surface
  chaussée rétrécie road narrows
  chaussée verglacée icy road
chaussette f sock
chaussure f shoe ; boot
chauve bald *(person)*
chauve-souris f bat *(creature)*
chef m chef ; chief ; head ; leader
  chef de train guard *(on train)*
chef-d'œuvre m masterpiece
chef-lieu m county town
chemin m path ; lane ; track ; way
  chemin de fer railway
cheminée f chimney; fireplace
chemise f shirt
  chemise de nuit nightdress
chemisier m blouse
chèque m cheque
  chèque de voyage traveller's cheque
cher(chère) dear ; expensive
chercher to look for
  aller chercher to fetch ; to collect
cheval m horse
  faire du cheval to ride *(horse)*
cheveux mpl hair
cheville f ankle
chèvre f goat
chevreau m kid *(goat, leather)*
chez at the house of
  chez moi at my home
chien m dog
chiffon m duster; rag
chips fpl crisps
chirurgien m surgeon
chocolat m chocolate ; hot chocolate
  chocolat à croquer plain chocolate
  chocolat au lait milk chocolate
choisir to choose
choix m range ; choice ; selection
chômage: au chômage unemployed

chope f tankard
chorale f choir
chose f thing
chou m cabbage
chou-fleur m cauliflower
CHU m hospital
chute f fall
cidre m cider
ciel m sky
cigare m cigar
cigarette f cigarette
cil m eyelash
cimetière m cemetery ; graveyard
cinéma m cinema
cintre m coat hanger
cirage m shoe polish
circuit m round trip ; circuit
circulation f traffic
cire f wax ; polish
cirque m circus
ciseaux mpl scissors
cité f city ; housing estate
citron m lemon
  citron vert lime
citronnade f still lemonade
clair(e) clear ; light
classe f grade ; class
clavicule f collar bone
clavier m keyboard
clé f key ; spanner
  clé de contact ignition key
  clé minute keys cut while you wait
clef f key
client(e) m/f client ; customer
clignotant m indicator *(on car)*
climatisation f air-conditioning
climatisé(e) air-conditioned
clinique f clinic *(private)*
cloche f bell *(church, school)*
clocher m steeple
clou m nail *(metal)*
  clou de girofle clove
club m club
cocher to tick
cochon m pig
cocktail m cocktail
cocotte f casserole dish
cocotte-minute f pressure cooker

code barres m barcode
code postal m postcode
cœur m heart
coffre-fort m strongbox ; safe
cognac m brandy
coiffeur m hairdresser ; barber
coiffeuse f hairdresser
coin m corner
coincé(e) jammed (stuck)
col m collar ; pass (in mountains)
colis m parcel
collant m tights
colle f glue
collège m secondary school
collègue m/f colleague
coller to stick ; to glue
collier m necklace ; dog collar
colline f hill
collision f crash (car)
colonne f column
  colonne vertébrale spine
combien how much/many
combinaison de plongée f wetsuit
  combinaison de ski ski suit
combustible m fuel
comédie f comedy
  comédie musicale musical
  (show)
commande f order (in restaurant)
commander to order
comme like
  comme ça like this
commencer to begin
comment? pardon? ; how? (in
  what way)
commerçant(e) m/f trader
commerce m commerce ; business ; trade
commissariat m police station
commode f chest of drawers
commotion f shock
  commotion (cérébrale) concussion
communication f communication ;
  call (on telephone)
communion f communion
compagne f girlfriend
compagnie f firm ; company

compagnon m boyfriend
compartiment m compartment
  (train)
complet(-ète) full (up)

COMPLET no vacancies

complètement quite (completely)
comporter to consist of
  se comporter to behave
composer (un numéro) to dial (a
  number)
composter to date stamp/punch
  (ticket)

COMPOSTER VOTRE BILLET
validate your ticket

comprenant including
comprendre to understand
comprimé m tablet
compris(e) included
  non compris not included
comptant m cash
compte m number ; account
  compte en banque bank account
compter to count (add up)
compteur m speedometer ; meter
comptoir m counter (in shop, etc)
comte m count ; earl
concert m concert
concierge m/f caretaker ; janitor
concours m contest ; aid
concurrent(e) m/f competitor
conducteur(-trice) m/f driver
conduire to drive
conduite f driving ; behaviour
confection f ready-to-wear clothes
conférence f conference
confession f confession
confirmer to confirm
confiserie f sweetshop
confiture f jam ; preserve
  confiture d'oranges marmalade
congélateur m freezer
congelé(e) frozen
connaître to know
conseil m advice ; council
conseiller to advise
conserver to keep
consigne f deposit

156

consigne automatique left luggage lockers

CONSIGNE left luggage

consommation f drink
consommé m clear soup
constat m report
constipé(e) constipated
construire to build
consulat m consulate
contacter to contact
contenir to contain
content(e) pleased
contenu m contents
continuer to continue
contraceptif m contraceptive
contrat m contract
  contrat de location lease
contravention f fine (penalty)
contre against ; versus
contre-filet m sirloin
contrôle m check
  contrôle des passeports passport control
  contrôle radar radar trap
contrôler to check
contrôleur(-euse) m/f ticket inspector
convenu(e) agreed
convoi m load
copie f copy (duplicate)
copier to copy
coque f shell ; cockle
coquelicot m poppy
coquet(te) pretty (place, etc)
coquillages mpl shellfish
coquille f shell
  coquille Saint-Jacques scallop
corail m coral ; type of train
corde f rope
  corde à linge clothes line
cordonnerie f shoe repair shop
cornet m cone
corniche f coast road
corps m body
correspondance f connection
correspondant(e) m/f penfriend
corrida f bull-fight
Corse f Corsica

costume m suit (man's)
côte f coast ; hill ; rib
  Côte d'Azur French Riviera
côté m side
  à côté de beside ; next to
côtelette f cutlet
coton m cotton
  coton hydrophile cotton wool
  coton-tige® cotton bud
cou m neck
couche (de bébé) f nappy
coucher du soleil m sunset
couchette f bunk ; berth
coude m elbow
coudre to sew
couette f continental quilt ; duvet
couler to run (water)
couleur f colour
coulis m purée
couloir m corridor ; aisle
coup m stroke ; shot ; blow
  coup de pied kick
  coup de soleil sunburn
  coup de téléphone phone call
coupe f goblet (ice cream)
  coupe (de cheveux) haircut
couper to cut
couple m couple (two people)
coupure f cut
  coupure de courant power cut
cour f court ; courtyard
courant m power ; current
courant(e) common ; current
courir to run
couronne f crown
courrier m mail ; post
  courrier électronique e-mail
courroie de ventilateur f fan belt
cours m lesson ; course ; rate
  cours particuliers private lessons
course f race (sport) ; errand
  course hippique horse race
  faire des courses to go shopping
court de tennis m tennis court
court(e) short
cousin(e) m/f cousin
coussin m cushion
coût m cost
couteau m knife

c

coûter to cost
coûteux(-euse) expensive
couture f sewing ; seam
couvent m convent ; monastery
couvercle m lid
couvert m cover charge ; place setting
  couverts cutlery
couvert(e) covered
couverture f blanket ; cover
crabe m crab
crapaud m toad
cravate f tie
crayon m pencil
crème f cream *(food, lotion)*
  crème à raser shaving cream
  crème aigre soured cream
  crème anglaise custard
  crème Chantilly whipped cream
  crème hydratante moisturizer
  crème pâtissière confectioner's custard
crémerie f dairy
crêpe f pancake
  crêpe fourrée stuffed pancake
crêperie f pancake shop/restaurant
cresson m watercress
crevaison f puncture
crevette f shrimp ; prawn
  crevette grise shrimp
  crevette rose prawn
cric m jack *(for car)*
crier to shout
crime m crime ; offence ; murder
crise f crisis ; attack *(medical)*
  crise cardiaque heart attack
cristal m crystal
crochet d'attelage m towbar
croire to believe
croisement m junction *(road)*
croisière f cruise
croix f cross
croquant(e) crisp ; crunchy
croque-madame m toasted cheese sandwich with ham and fried egg
croque-monsieur m toasted ham and cheese sandwich

croustade f pastry shell with filling
croûte f crust
cru(e) raw
crudités fpl raw vegetables
crue subite f flash flood
crustacé m shellfish
cube de bouillon m stock cube
cuiller f spoon
  cuiller à café teaspoon
cuir m leather
cuisiné(e) cooked
cuisine f cooking ; cuisine ; kitchen
  cuisine familiale home cooking
  faire la cuisine to cook
cuisiner to cook *(do cooking)*
cuisinier m cook
cuisinière f cook ; cooker
cuisse f thigh
  cuisses de grenouille frogs' legs
cuit(e) cooked ; well done *(steak)*
cuivre m copper
  cuivre jaune brass
culotte f panties
culturisme m body-building
curieux(-euse) funny *(strange)*
curseur m cursor *(computer)*
cuvée f vintage
  cuvée du patron house wine
cuvette f washing up bowl
cyclisme m cycling
cygne m swan
cystite f cystitis

D

dactylo m/f typist
daltonien(ne) colour-blind
dame f lady

  DAMES ladies

danger m danger
dangereux(-euse) dangerous
dans into ; in ; on
danser to dance
date f date *(day)*
  date de naissance date of birth
  date limite de vente sell-by date
daube f stew

de from ; of; any see **GRAMMAR**
dé m dice
début m beginning
débutant(e) m/f beginner
décaféiné(e) decaffeinated

DÉCEMBRE December

décès m death
décharge f electric shock
  décharge publique rubbish dump
déchargement m unloading
déchirer to rip
déci m 1 decilitre of wine (Switz.)
déclaration f statement ; report
  déclaration de douane customs declaration
décollage m takeoff
décoller to take off (plane)
décolleté m low neck
décongeler to defrost
décontracté(e) relaxed ; casual
découvrir to discover
décrire to describe
décrocher to lift the receiver
dedans inside
dédouaner to clear customs
défaire to unfasten ; to unpack
défaut m fault ; defect
défectueux(-euse) faulty

DÉFENSE DE... no...

  défense de fumer no smoking
  défense de stationner no parking
dégâts mpl damage
dégeler to thaw
dégivrer to de-ice (windscreen)
dégustation f tasting

DÉGUSTATION DES VINS wine tasting

dehors outside ; outdoors
déjeuner m lunch
délicieux(-euse) delicious
délit m offence
deltaplane m hang-glider
demain tomorrow
demande f application ; request
  demandes d'emploi situations wanted

demander to ask (for)
démaquillant m make-up remover
démarqué(e) reduced (goods)
démarreur m starter (in car)
demi(e) half
demi-pension f half board
demi-sec medium-dry
demi-tarif m half fare
demi-tour m U-turn
dent f tooth
dentelle f lace
dentier m dentures
dentifrice m toothpaste
dentiste m/f dentist
déodorant m deodorant
dépannage m breakdown service
dépanneuse f breakdown van
départ m departure

DÉPARTS departures

département m regional division
dépasser to exceed ; to overtake
dépenses fpl expenditure
dépliant m brochure
dépôt m deposit ; depot
  dépôt d'ordures rubbish dump
dépression f depression ; nervous breakdown
depuis since
déranger to disturb
dernier(-ère) last ; latest
derrière at the back ; behind
derrière m bottom (buttocks)
dès from ; since
  dès votre arrivée as soon as you arrive
désagréable unpleasant
descendre to go down ; to get off
description f description
déshabiller to undress
  se déshabiller to undress oneself
désirer to want
désistement m withdrawal
désodorisant m air freshener
désolé(e) sorry
desserré(e) loose (not fastened)
dessert m pudding
dessin m drawing
  dessin animé cartoon (animated)

d

dessous underneath
dessus on top
destinataire *m/f* addressee
destination *f* destination
  à destination de bound for
détail *m* detail
  au détail retail
détergent *m* detergent
détourner to divert
deux two
  deux fois twice
  les deux both
deuxième second
devant in front (of)
développer to develop
devenir to become

DÉVIATION diversion

devis *m* quotation (price)
devises *fpl* currency
dévisser to unscrew
devoir to have to; to owe
diabète *m* diabetes
diabétique diabetic
diamant *m* diamond
diaphragme *m* cap (contraceptive)
diapositive *f* slide (photograph)
diarrhée *f* diarrhoea
dictionnaire *m* dictionary
diététique dietary ; health foods
différent(e) different
difficile difficult
digue *f* dyke ; jetty

DIMANCHE Sunday

dinde *f* turkey
dîner to have dinner
dîner *m* dinner ; lunch (Switz./Belg.)
  dîner spectacle cabaret dinner
dire to say ; to tell
direct: train direct through train
directeur *m* manager ; headmaster
direction *f* management ; direction
directrice *f* manageress ; head-mistress
discothèque *f* disco
discussion *f* argument
disjoncteur *m* circuit breaker
disloquer to dislocate

disparaître to disappear
disparu(e) missing (disappeared)
disponible available
disque *m* record ; disk (computer)
  disque de stationnement parking disk
  disque dur hard disk
disquette *f* floppy disk
dissolvant *m* nail polish remover
distractions *fpl* entertainment
distributeur *m* dispenser
  distributeur automatique vending machine ; cash machine
divers(e) various
divertissements *mpl* entertainment
divorcé(e) divorced
docteur *m* doctor
doigt *m* finger
  doigt de pied toe
domestique *m/f* servant ; maid
domicile *m* home ; address
donner to give ; to give away
doré(e) golden
dormir to sleep
  dormir tard to sleep in
dos *m* back (of body)
dossier *m* file (for papers)
douane *f* customs
double double
doubler to overtake
douche *f* shower
douleur *f* pain
douloureux(-euse) painful
doux (douce) mild ; gentle ; soft ; sweet
douzaine *f* dozen
dragée *f* sugared almond
drap *m* sheet
drapeau *m* flag
drogue *f* drug
droguerie *f* hardware shop
droit *m* right (entitlement)
droit(e) right (not left) ; straight
droite *f* right-hand side
  à droite on/to the right
  tenez votre droite keep to right
dur(e) hard ; hard-boiled ; tough
durée *f* length (of time or stay)

E

eau f water
  eau de Javel bleach
  eau dentifrice mouthwash
  eau douce fresh water *(not salt)*
  eau du robinet tap-water
  eau minérale mineral water

  EAU POTABLE drinking water

  eau salée salt water
eau-de-vie brandy
ébène f ebony
échanger to exchange
échantillon m sample
échapper to escape
écharpe f scarf *(woollen)*
échelle f ladder
  échelle de secours fire escape
éclairage m lighting
éclairs mpl lightning
écluse f lock *(in canal)*
école f school
  école maternelle nursery school
écorce f peel *(of orange, lemon)*
écossais(e) Scottish
Écosse f Scotland
écouter to listen to
écouteur m receiver
écran m screen
  écran solaire sunscreen *(lotion)*
  écran total sunblock
écrire to write
écrivain m author
écrou m nut *(for bolt)*
écurie f stable
édulcorant m sweetener
église f church
élastique m elastic band
électricien m electrician
électrique electric
élément m unit ; element
emballer to wrap (up)
embarcadère m jetty *(landing pier)*
embarquement m boarding
embouteillage m traffic jam
embrasser to kiss
embrayage m clutch *(in car)*

émission f programme ; broadcast
emploi m use ; job
emporter to take away
emprunter to borrow
en some ; any ; in ; to ; made of
  en cas de in case of
  en face de opposite
  en gros in bulk ; wholesale

  EN PANNE out of order

  en retard late
  en train/voiture by train/ car
encaisser to cash *(cheque)*
enceinte pregnant
enchanté(e)! pleased to meet you!
encore still ; yet ; again
encre f ink
endommager to damage
endroit m place ; spot
enfant m/f child
enfler to swell *(bump, eye, etc)*
enlever to take away ; to take off
(clothes)
  enlever le haut to go topless
enneigé(e) snowed up
ennui m boredom ; nuisance ;
trouble
ennuyeux boring
enregistrement m check-in desk
enregistrer to record ; to check
in ; to video
enseignement m education
enseigner to teach
ensemble together
ensuite next ; after that
entendre to hear
entier(-ère) whole
entorse f sprain
entracte m interval
entre between
entrecôte f rib steak
entrée f admission ; starter *(food)*

  ENTRÉE entrance

  entrée gratuite admission free
  entrée interdite no entry
entrepôt m warehouse
entrepreneur m contractor
entreprise f firm ; company

entrer to come in ; to go in
entretien m maintenance ; interview
entrevue f interview
entrez! come in!
enveloppe f envelope
  enveloppe matelassée padded envelope
envers: l'envers wrong side
  à l'envers upside down ; back to front
environ around ; about
environs mpl surroundings
envoyer to send
épais(se) thick
épargner to save (money)
épaule f shoulder
épi m ear (of corn)
  épi de maïs corn-on-the-cob
épice f spice
épicerie f grocer's shop
  épicerie fine delicatessen
épilation f hair removal
  épilation à la cire f waxing
épileptique epileptic
épinards mpl spinach
épine f thorn
épingle f pin
  épingle de sûreté safety pin
éponge f sponge
époque f age
  d'époque period (furniture)
épouvantail m scarecrow
épreuve f event (sports) ; print
épuisé(e) sold out ; out of stock ; used up
épuiser to use up ; to run out of
  s'épuiser to run out
équipage m crew
équipe f team ; shift
équipement m equipment
équitation f horse-riding
erreur f mistake
escalade f climbing
escalator m escalator
escalier m stairs
  escalier de secours fire escape
  escalier mécanique escalator
escargot m snail

escarpement m cliff (in mountains)
Espagne f Spain
espagnol(e) Spanish
espèce f sort
espérer to hope
esquimau m ice lolly
essai m trial ; test
essayer to try ; to try on
essence f petrol
  essence sans plomb unleaded petrol
essorer to spin(-dry) ; to wring
essoreuse f spin dryer
essuie-glace m windscreen wipers
essuie-tout m kitchen paper
esthétique f beauty salon
estivants mpl summer holiday-makers
estomac m stomach
estragon m tarragon
et and
étage m storey
  dernier étage the top floor
étain m tin ; pewter
étang m pond
étape f stage
état m state
  États Unis United States
été m summer
éteindre to turn off
éteint(e) out (light)
éternuer to sneeze
étiquette f label
  étiquette à bagages luggage tag
étoile f star
étranger(-ère) m/f foreigner
  à l'étranger overseas ; abroad
être see (to be) **GRAMMAR**
étroit(e) narrow ; tight
étudiant(e) m/f student
étudier to study
étui m case (camera, glasses)
eurochèque m eurocheque
Europe f Europe
européen(ne) European
eux them
évanoui(e) fainted
  s'évanouir to faint
événement m occasion ; event

éventail m fan (handheld)
éventé(e) flat (beer)
évêque m bishop
évier m sink (washbasin)
éviter to avoid
exact(e) right (correct)
examen m examination
excédent de bagages m excess baggage
excellent(e) excellent
excès de vitesse m speeding
excursion f trip ; outing ; excursion
excuses fpl apologies
excusez-moi! excuse me!
exemplaire m copy
exercice m exercise
expéditeur m sender
expert(e) m/f expert
expirer to expire (ticket, passport)
expliquer to explain
exporter to export
exposition f exhibition
exprès on purpose ; deliberately
  en exprès express (parcel, etc)
extérieur(e) outside
extincteur m fire extinguisher
extra top-quality ; first-rate

F

fabrication f manufacturing
fabriquer manufacture
  fabriqué en... made in...
face: en face (de) opposite
fâché(e) angry
facile easy
façon f way ; manner
facteur(-trice) m/f postman
facture f invoice
  facture détaillée itemized bill
faible weak
faïence f earthenware
faim f hunger
  avoir faim hungry: to be hungry
faire to make ; to do
  faire du stop to hitchhike
faisan m pheasant
fait main handmade
falaise f cliff (along coast)

famille f family
farci(e) stuffed
fard à paupières m eye shadow
farine f flour
fatigué(e) tired
fausse couche f miscarriage
faute f mistake ; foul (football)
fauteuil m armchair ; seat
  fauteuil roulant wheelchair
faux (fausse) fake ; false ; wrong
fax m fax
faxer to fax
félicitations fpl congratulations
femme f woman ; wife
  femme au foyer housewife
  femme d'affaires businesswoman
  femme de chambre chambermaid
  femme de ménage cleaner
  femme policier police woman
fenêtre f window
fenouil m fennel
fente f crack ; slot
fer m iron (material, golf club)
  fer à repasser iron (for clothes)
féra f freshwater fish (Switz.)
férié(e): jour férié public holiday
ferme f farmhouse ; farm

FERMÉ closed

fermer to close/shut ; to turn off
  fermer à clé to lock
fermeture f closing
  fermeture Éclair® zip
ferroviaire railway ; rail
ferry m car ferry
fête f holiday ; fête ; party
  fête des rois Epiphany
  fête foraine funfair
feu m fire ; traffic lights
  feu (de joie) bonfire (celebration)
  feu d'artifice fireworks
  feu de position sidelight
  feu rouge red light
feuille f leaf ; sheet (of paper)
feuilleton m soap opera
feutre m felt ; felt-tip pen

FÉVRIER February

fiancé(e) engaged (to be married)

f

ficelle f string ; thin French stick
fiche f token; form slip (of paper)
fichier m file (computer)
fièvre f fever
  avoir de la fièvre to have a
  temperature
figue f fig
fil m thread ; lead (electrical)
  fil dentaire dental floss
file f lane ; row
filet m net ; fillet (of meat, fish)
  filet à bagages luggage rack
fille f daughter ; girl
film m film
fils m son
filtre m filter (on cigarette)
  filtre à huile oil filter
fin f end
fin(e) thin (material) ; fine (delicate)
fini(e) finished
finir to end ; to finish
fixer to fix (make firm)
flacon m bottle (small)
flamand(e) Flemish
flan m sweet tart
flash m flash (for camera)
fleur f flower
fleuriste m/f florist
fleuve m river
flipper m pinball
flocon m flake
flûte f long, thin loaf
foie m liver
  foie gras goose liver
foire f fair
  foire à/aux... special offer on...
fois f time
  cette fois this time
  une fois once
folle mad
foncé(e) dark (colour)
fonctionner to work (machine)
fond m back (of hall, room) ; bottom
fondre to melt
force f strength
forêt f forest
forfait m fixed price ; ski pass
forme f shape ; style
formidable great (wonderful)

formulaire m form (document)
fort(e) loud; strong
forteresse f fort
fosse f pit ; grave
  fosse septique septic tank
fou (folle) mad ; crazy (prices)
fouetté(e) whipped (cream, eggs)
foulard m scarf (headscarf)
foule f crowd
four m oven
  four à micro-ondes microwave
fourchette f fork
fournir to supply
fourré(e) filled ; fur-lined
fourrure f fur
fraîche fresh ; cool ; wet (paint)
frais fresh ; cool
frais mpl costs ; expenses
fraise f strawberry
framboise f raspberry
français(e) French
Français(e) Frenchman/woman
frapper to hit; to knock (on door)
frein m brake
freiner to brake
fréquent(e) frequent
frère m brother
fret m freight (goods)
frigo m fridge
frisé(e) curly
frit(e) fried
friterie f chip shop
frites fpl french fries ; chips
friture f small fried fish

FROID cold

fromage m cheese
froment m wheat
front m forehead
frontière f border ; boundary
frotter to rub
fruit m fruit
  fruits de mer seafood
  fruits secs dried fruit
fuite f leak
fumé(e) smoked
fumée f smoke
fumer to smoke

FUMEURS smokers

fumier m manure
funiculaire m funicular railway
fuseau m ski pants
fusible m fuse
fusil m gun

G

gagner to earn; to win
galerie f art gallery ; arcade ;
  roof-rack
gallois(e) Welsh
gambas fpl large prawns
gant m glove
  gant de toilette face cloth
  gants de ménage rubber gloves
garage m garage
garantie f guarantee
garçon m boy ; waiter
garde f custody; guard
  garde-côte coastguard
garder to keep ; to look after
gardien(ne) m/f caretaker ; warden
gare f railway station
  gare routière bus terminal
garer to park
garni(e) served with vegetables
  or chips
gas-oil m diesel fuel
gâteau m cake ; gateau
gauche left
  à gauche to/on the left
gaucher(-ère) left-handed
gaz m gas
  gaz d'échappement exhaust
  fumes
gaz-oil m diesel fuel
gazeux(-euse) fizzy
gel m frost
  gel pour cheveux hair gel
gelé(e) frozen
gelée f jelly ; aspic
gênant inconvenient
gendarme m policeman
gendarmerie f police station
gendre m son-in-law

généreux(-euse) generous
genou m knee
gentil(-ille) kind (person)
gérant(e) m/f manager/manageress
gérer to manage (be in charge of)
gibier m game (hunting)
gilet m waistcoat
  gilet de sauvetage life jacket
gingembre m ginger
gîte m self-catering house/flat
glace f ice ; ice cream ; mirror
glacé(e) chilled ; iced
glacier m glacier ; ice-cream maker
glacière f cool-box (for picnic)
glaçon m ice cube
glissant(e) slippery
glisser to slip
gomme f rubber (eraser)
gorge f throat ; gorge
gosse m/f kid (child)
gothique Gothic
goût m flavour ; taste
goûter to taste
grain de beauté m mole (on skin)
graine f seed
gramme m gram
grand(e) great ; high (speed,
  number) ; big ; tall
grand-mère f grandmother
grand-père m grandfather
Grande-Bretagne f Great Britain
grands-parents mpl grandparents
grange f barn
granité m flavoured crushed ice
grappe f bunch (of grapes)
gras(se) fat ; greasy
gratis free
gratuit(e) free of charge
grave serious
gravure f print (picture)
grêle f hail
grenier m attic
grenouille f frog
grève f strike (industrial)
grillé(e) grilled
grille-pain m toaster
Grèce f Greece
grippe f flu
gris(e) grey

g

gros(se) big ; large ; fat
gros lot m jackpot
grotte f cave
groupe m group ; party ; band
  groupe sanguin blood group
guêpe f wasp
guerre f war
gueule de bois f hangover

GUICHET ticket office

guide m guide ; guidebook
  guide de conversation phrase book
guidon m handlebars
guitare f guitar

H

H = heure
habillé(e) dressed
habiller to dress
  s'habiller to get dressed
habitant(e) m/f inhabitant

habiter to live (in a place)
habituel(le) usual ; regular
haché(e) minced
  steak haché m hamburger
hachis m minced meat
halles fpl central food market
hamburger m burger
hameçon m hook (fishing)
hanche f hip
handicapé(e) disabled (person)
haricot m bean
haut m top (of ladder, bikini etc)
  en haut upstairs
haut(e) high ; tall
hauteur f height
hebdomadaire weekly
hébergement m lodging
hépatite f hepatitis
herbe f grass
  fines herbes herbs
hernie f hernia
heure f hour ; time of day
  à l'heure on time
  heure de pointe rush hour
heureux(-euse) happy
hibou m owl

hier yesterday
hippisme m horse riding
hippodrome m racecourse
hirondelle f swallow (bird)
historique historic
hiver m winter
hollandais(e) Dutch
homard m lobster
homéopathie f homeopathy
homme m man
  homme au foyer househusband
  homme d'affaires businessman

HOMMES gents

homo m gay (person)
honnête honest
honoraires mpl fee
hôpital m hospital
horaire m timetable ; schedule
horloge f clock
hors: hors de out of
  hors service out of order
  hors-taxe duty-free
  hors-saison off-season
hôte m host ; guest
hôtel m hotel
  hôtel de ville town hall
hôtesse f stewardess
huile f oil
  huile d'olive olive oil
  huile d'arachide groundnut oil
  huile de tournesol sunflower oil
huître f oyster
hypermarché m hypermarket
hypermétrope long sighted
hypertension f high blood pressure

I

ici here
idée f idea
il y a... there is/are...
  il y a un défaut there's a fault
  il y a une semaine a week ago
île f island
illimité(e) unlimited
immédiatement immediately
immeuble m building (offices, flats)
immunisation f immunisation

impair(e) odd *(number)*
impasse *f* dead end
imperméable waterproof
important(e) important
importer to import
impossible impossible
impôt *m* tax
imprimer to print
incendie *m* fire
inclu(e) included ; inclusive
inconfortable uncomfortable
incorrect(e) wrong
indicateur *m* guide ; timetable
indicatif *m* dialling code
indications *fpl* instructions ; directions
indigestion *f* indigestion
indispensable essential
infectieux(-euse) infectious
infection *f* infection
inférieur(e) inferior ; lower
infirmerie *f* infirmary
infirmier(-ière) *m/f* nurse
informations *fpl* news ; information
infusion *f* herbal tea
ingénieur *m/f* engineer
ingrédient *m* ingredient
inhalateur *m* inhaler
inondation *f* flood
inquiet(-iète) worried
inscrire to write (down) ; to enrol
insecte *m* insect
insolation *f* sunstroke
installations *fpl* facilities
instant *m* moment
  un instant! just a minute!
institut *m* institute
  institut de beauté beauty salon
insuline *f* insulin
intelligent(e) intelligent

INTERDIT DE no...

intéressant(e) interesting
intérieur: à l'intérieur indoors
international(e) international
interprète *m/f* interpreter
intervention *f* operation *(surgical)*
intoxication alimentaire *f* food poisoning

introduire to introduce ; to insert
inutile useless ; unnecessary
invalide *m/f* disabled person
invité(e) *m/f* guest *(house guest)*
inviter to invite
irlandais(e) Irish
Irlande *f* Ireland
Irlande du Nord *f* Northern Ireland
issue de secours *f* emergency exit
Italie *f* Italy
italien(ne) Italian
itinéraire *m* route
  itinéraire touristique scenic route
ivoire *m* ivory
ivre drunk

J

jaloux(-ouse) jealous
jamais never
jambe *f* leg
jambon *m* ham

JANVIER January

Japon *m* Japan
jardin *m* garden
jauge (de niveau d'huile) *f* dipstick
jaune yellow
jaune d'œuf *m* egg yolk
jaunisse *f* jaundice
jetable disposable
jetée *f* pier
jeter to throw
jeton *m* token
jeu *m* game ; set *(of tools, etc)* ; gambling
  jeu électronique computer game
  jeu vidéo video game
  jeu-concours quiz

JEUDI Thursday

jeune young
jeunesse *f* youth
joindre to join ; to enclose
joli(e) pretty
jonquille *f* daffodil
joue *f* cheek
jouer to play *(games)*
jouet *m* toy

j

jour m day
  jour férié public holiday
journal m newspaper
journaliste m/f journalist
journée f day *(length of time)*
juge m judge
juif (juive) Jewish

JUILLET July

JUIN June

jumeaux mpl twins
jumelé(e) avec... twinned with...
jumelles fpl twins ; binoculars
jupe f skirt
jus m juice
  jus d'orange orange juice
  jus de fruit fruit juice
  jus de viande gravy
jusqu'à until ; till
juste fair *(not unfair)*

K

k

kart m go-cart
kas(c)her kosher
kayak m canoe
kilo m kilo(gram)
kilométrage m = mileage
  kilométrage illimité unlimited mileage
kilomètre m kilometre
kiosque m kiosk ; newsstand
klaxonner to sound one's horn
kyste m cyst

L

l

là there
lac m lake
lacets mpl shoelaces
laid(e) ugly
laine f wool
  laine polaire fleece *(top/jacket)*
laisse f leash
laisser to leave
  laissez en blanc leave blank

lait m milk
  lait démaquillant cleansing milk
  lait demi-écrémé semi-skimmed milk
  lait écrémé skim(med) milk
  lait entier full-cream milk
  lait longue conservation long-life milk
  lait maternisé baby milk *(formula)*
  lait solaire suntan lotion
laiterie f dairy
laitue f lettuce
lame f blade
  lames de rasoir razor blades
lampe f light ; lamp
  lampe de poche torch
landau m pram ; baby carriage
langue f tongue ; language
lapin m rabbit
laque f hair spray
lard m fat ; *(streaky)* bacon
large wide ; broad
largeur f width
laurier m sweet bay ; bay leaves
lavable washable
lavabo m washbasin
  lavabos toilets
lavage m washing
lavande f lavender
lave-auto m car wash
lave-glace m screen wash
lave-linge m washing machine
laver to wash
  se laver to wash oneself
laverie automatique f launderette
lave-vaisselle m dishwasher
laxatif m laxative
layette f baby clothes
leçon f lesson
  leçons particulières private lessons
lecture f reading
  lecture sur les lèvres lip-reading
légal(e) legal
léger(-ère) light ; weak *(tea, etc)*
légume m vegetable
lendemain m next day
lent(e) slow
lentement slowly

lentille f lentil ; lens (of glasses)
  lentille de contact contact lens
lesbienne f lesbian
lessive f soap powder ; washing
lettre f letter
  lettre recommandée registered letter
leur(s) (to them) ; their
levain m yeast
levée f collection (of mail)
lever to lift
  se lever to get up (out of bed)
lever du soleil m sunrise
lèvre f lip
levure f yeast
libellule f dragonfly
librairie f bookshop

LIBRE free/vacant

LIBRE-SERVICE self-service

lieu m place (location)
lièvre m hare
ligne f line ; service ; route
lime à ongles f nail file
limitation de vitesse f speed limit
limonade f lemonade
lin m linen (cloth)
linge m linen (bed, table) ; laundry
lingerie f lingerie
lingettes fpl baby wipes
lion m lion
liquide f liquid
  liquide de freins brake fluid
lire to read
liste f list
lit m bed
  lit d'enfant cot
  lit simple single bed
  lits jumeaux twin beds
  grand lit double bed
litre m litre
livraison f delivery (of goods)
  livraison des bagages baggage reclaim
livre f pound
livre m book
local(e) local
locataire m/f tenant ; lodger

location f hiring (out) ; letting
logement m accommodation
loger to stay (reside for while)
logiciel m computer software
loi f law
loin far
lointain(e) distant
loisir m leisure
Londres London
long(ue) long
  le long de along
longe f loin (of meat)
longtemps for a long time
longueur f length
lot m prize ; lot (at auction)
loterie f lottery
lotion f lotion
loto m numerical lottery
lotte f monkfish ; angler fish
louer to let ; to hire ; to rent

À LOUER for hire/to rent

loup m wolf ; sea perch
loupe f magnifying glass
lourd(e) heavy
loyer m rent
luge f sledge ; toboggan
lumière f light

LUNDI Monday

lune f moon
  lune de miel honeymoon
lunettes fpl glasses
  lunettes de soleil sunglasses
  lunettes protectrices goggles
luxe m luxury
lycée m secondary school

M

M sign for the Paris metro
machine f machine
  machine à laver washing machine
mâchoire f jaw
Madame f Mrs ; Ms ; Madam
madeleine f small sponge cake
Mademoiselle f Miss
madère m Madeira (wine)
magasin m shop

m

grand magasin department store
magnétophone m tape recorder
magnétoscope m video-cassette recorder
magret de canard m breast fillet of duck

MAI May

maigre lean *(meat)*
maigrir to slim
maillet m mallet
maillot m vest
  maillot de bain swimsuit
main f hand
maintenant now
maire m mayor
mairie f town hall
mais but
maison f house ; home
  maison de campagne villa
maître d'hôtel m head waiter
majuscule f capital letter
mal badly

m

mal m harm ; pain
  mal aux dents toothache
  mal de mer seasickness
  mal de tête headache
  faire du mal à quelqu'un to harm someone
malade sick *(ill)*
malade m/f sick person ; patient
maladie f disease
malentendu m misunderstanding
malle f trunk *(luggage)*
maman f mummy
manche m sleeve
Manche f the Channel
mandat m money order
manger to eat
manière f way *(manner)*
manifestation f demonstration
manque m shortage ; lack
manteau m coat
maquereau m mackerel
maquillage m make-up
marais m marsh
marbre m marble *(material)*
marc m white grape spirit

marchand m dealer ; merchant
  marchand de poisson fishmonger
  marchand de vin wine merchant
marche f step ; march; walking
  marche arrière reverse gear
marché m market
  marché aux puces flea market
marcher to walk; to work *(machine, car)*
  en marche on *(machine)*

MARDI Tuesday

mardi gras Shrove Tuesday
marée f tide
  marée basse low tide
  marée haute high tide
margarine f margarine
mari m husband
mariage m wedding
marié m bridegroom
marié(e) married
mariée f bride
marier to marry
  se marier to get married
mariné(e) marinated
marionnette f puppet
marque f make ; brand *(name)*
marquer to score *(goal, point)*
marron brown
marron m chestnut

MARS March

marteau m hammer
masculin male *(person, on forms)*
mât m mast
match de football m football match
match en nocturne m floodlit fixture
matelas m mattress
  matelas pneumatique lilo®
matériel m equipment ; kit
matin m morning
mauvais(e) bad ; wrong ; off *(food)*
maximum m maximum
mazout m oil *(for heating)*
mécanicien m mechanic
mécanique manual *(gear change)*
médecin m doctor

médicament m medicine ; drug ; medication
médiéval(e) medieval
Méditérranée f Mediterranean Sea
méduse f jellyfish
meilleur(e) best ; better
 meilleurs vœux best wishes
membre m member (of club, etc)
même same
mémoire f memory
ménage m housework
méningite f meningitis
mensuel(le) monthly
menthe f mint ; mint tea
menton m chin
menu m menu (set)
 menu à prix fixe set price menu
mer f sea
 mer du Nord North Sea
mercerie f haberdasher's
merci thank you

MERCREDI Wednesday

mère f mother
merlan m whiting
merlu m hake
mérou m grouper
merveilleux(-euse) wonderful
message m message
messe f mass (church)
messieurs mpl men

MESSIEURS gents

mesure f measurement
mesurer to measure
métal m metal
météo f weather forecast
métier m trade ; occupation ; craft
mètre m metre
 mètre à ruban tape measure
métro m underground railway
mettre to put ; to put on
 mettre au point focus (camera)
 mettre en marche to turn on
meublé(e) furnished
meubles mpl furniture
 meubles de style period furniture
mi-bas mpl pop-socks ; knee-highs
midi m midday ; noon

Midi m the south of France
miel m honey
mieux better ; best
migraine f headache ; migraine
milieu m middle
mille m thousand
millimètre m millimetre
million m million
mince slim ; thin
mine f expression ; mine (coal, etc)
mineur m miner
mineur(e) under age ; minor
minicassette f cassette player
minimum m minimum
minuit m midnight
minuscule tiny
minute f minute
minuteur m timer
mirabelle f plum ; plum brandy
miroir m mirror
mise en plis f set (for hair)
mistral m strong cold dry wind
mite f moth (clothes)
mixte mixed
mobilier m furniture
mode f fashion
 à la mode fashionable
 mode d'emploi instructions for use
modem m modem
moderne modern
moelle f marrow (beef, etc)
moi me
moineau m sparrow
moins less ; minus
 moins (de) less (than)
 moins cher cheaper
moins m the least
mois m month
moisissure f mould (fungus)
moitié f half
 à moitié prix half-price
moka m coffee cream cake ; mocha coffee
molle soft
moment m moment
 en ce moment at the moment
mon/ma/mes my see GRAMMAR
monastère m monastery

m

monde m world ; people
moniteur m instructor ; coach
monitrice f instructress ; coach
monnaie f currency ; change (money)
monnayeur m automatic change machine
monsieur m gentleman
Monsieur m Mr ; sir
montagne f mountain
montant m amount (total)
monter to take up ; to go up ; to rise; to get in (car)
　monter à cheval to horse-ride
montre f watch
montrer to show
monument m monument
moquette f fitted carpet
morceau m piece ; bit ; cut (of meat)
mordu(e) bitten
morsure f bite
　morsure de serpent snake bite
mort(e) dead
mosquée f mosque
mot m word ; note (letter)
　mot de passe password
　mots croisés crossword puzzle
motel m motel
moteur m engine ; motor
motif m pattern
moto f motorbike
mou (molle) soft
mouche f fly
moucheron m midge
mouchoir m handkerchief
mouette f seagull
mouillé(e) wet
moule f mussel
moulin m mill
　moulin à vent windmill
moulinet m reel (fishing)
mourir to die
mousse f foam ; mousse
　mousse à raser shaving foam
　mousse coiffante hair mousse
mousseux(-euse) sparkling (wine)
moustache f moustache
moustiquaire f mosquito net
moustique m mosquito

moutarde f mustard
mouton m sheep ; lamb or mutton
moyen(ne) average
moyenne f average
muguet m lily of the valley ; thrush (candida)
muni(e) de supplied with ; in possession of
mur m wall
mûr(e) mature ; ripe
mûre f blackberry
muscade f nutmeg
muscle m muscle
musée m museum ; art gallery
　musée d'art art gallery
musique f music
myope short-sighted
myrtille f bilberry

N

nager to swim
naissance f birth
nappe f tablecloth
nappé(e) coated (with chocolate, etc)
natation f swimming
national(e) national
nationalité f nationality
natte f plait
nature f wildlife
naturel(le) natural
nautique nautical ; water
navette f shuttle (bus service)
navigation f sailing
navire m ship
né(e) born
négatif m negative (photography)
neige f snow
neiger to snow
nettoyage m cleaning
　nettoyage à sec dry-cleaning
nettoyer to clean
neuf (neuve) new
neveu m nephew
névralgie f headache
nez m nose
niche f kennel
nid m nest
　nid de poule pothole

nièce f niece
niveau m level ; standard
noce f wedding
nocturne m late opening
Noël m Christmas
  joyeux Noël! merry Christmas!
noir(e) black
noisette f hazelnut
noix f nut ; walnut
nom m name ; noun
  nom de famille family name
  nom de jeune fille maiden name
nombre m number
nombreux(-euse) numerous
non no ; not
non alcoolisé(e) non-alcoholic
non-fumeur non-smoking

nord m north
normal(e) normal ; standard *(size)*
nos our
notaire m solicitor
note f note ; bill ; memo
notre our
nœud m knot
nourrir to feed
nourriture f food
nouveau (nouvelle) new
  de nouveau again
nouvelles fpl news

noyer m walnut tree
nu(e) naked ; bare
nuage m cloud
nuageux(-euse) cloudy
nucléaire nuclear
nuit f night
  bonne nuit good night
numéro m number ; act ; issue

O

objectif m objective ; lens *(of camera)*
objet m object
  objets de valeur valuable items
  objets trouvés lost property

obligatoire compulsory
obsèques fpl funeral
obtenir to get ; to obtain
occasion f occasion ; bargain
occupé(e) busy ; hired *(taxi)*

océan m ocean

odeur f smell
œuf m egg
  œuf de Pâques Easter egg
office m service *(church)* ; office
  office du tourisme tourist office
offre f offer
oie f goose
oignon m onion
œil m eye
œillet m carnation
oiseau m bird
olive f olive
ombre f shade/shadow
  à l'ombre in the shade
oncle m uncle
onde f wave
ongle m nail *(finger)*
opéra m opera
or m gold
orage m storm
orange orange ; amber *(traffic light)*
orange f orange
orangeade f orange squash
orchestre m orchestra ; stalls *(in theatre)*
ordinaire ordinary
ordinateur m computer
ordonnance f prescription
ordre m order
  à l'ordre de payable to
ordures fpl litter *(rubbish)*
oreille f ear
oreiller m pillow
oreillons mpl mumps
organiser to organize
orge f barley
origan m oregano
os m bone
oseille f sorrel

173

osier m wicker
ou or
où where
oublier to forget
ouest m west
oui yes
ours(e) m/f bear (animal)
oursin m sea urchin
outils mpl tools
ouvert(e) open ; on (tap, gas, etc)

OUVERT open

ouverture f overture ; opening
ouvrable working (day)
ouvre-boîtes m can opener
ouvre-bouteilles m bottle opener
ouvrir to open

P

page f page
  pages jaunes Yellow Pages
paiement m payment
paille f straw
pain m bread ; loaf of bread
  pain bis brown bread
  pain complet wholemeal bread
  pain grillé toast
pair(e) even
paire f pair
paix f peace
palais m palace
pâle pale
palmes fpl flippers
palourde f clam
pamplemousse m grapefruit
panaché m shandy
pané(e) in breadcrumbs
panier m basket
  panier repas packed lunch
panne f breakdown
panneau m sign
pansement m bandage
pantalon m trousers
pantoufles fpl slippers
pape m pope
papeterie f stationer's shop
papier m paper
  papier à lettres writing paper

papier alu(minium) foil
  papier cadeau gift-wrap
  papier hygiénique toilet paper
  papiers identity papers ; driving licence
papillon m butterfly
pâquerette f daisy
Pâques m or fpl Easter
paquet m package ; pack ; packet
par by ; through ; per
  par example for example
  par jour per day
  par téléphone by phone
  par voie orale take by mouth (medicine)
paradis m heaven
paralysé(e) paralysed
parapluie m umbrella
parasol m sunshade
parc m park
  parc d'attractions funfair
parce que because
parcmètre m parking meter
pardon! sorry! ; excuse me!
parer to ward off
pare-brise m windscreen
pare-chocs m bumper
parent(e) m/f relative
parents mpl parents
paresseux(-euse) lazy
parfait(e) perfect
parfum m perfume ; flavour
parfumerie f perfume shop
pari m bet
  faire un pari sur to bet on
parking m car park
  parking assuré parking facilities
  parking souterrain underground car park
  parking surveillé attended car park
parler (avec) to speak (to) ; to talk (to)
paroisse f parish
partager to share
parterre m flowerbed
parti m political party
partie f part ; match (game)
partir to leave ; to go

à partir de from
partout everywhere
pas not
  pas encore not yet
pas m step ; pace
passage m passage
  passage à niveau level crossing
  passage clouté pedestrian crossing
  passage interdit no through way
  passage souterrain underpass
passager(-ère) m/f passenger
passé(e) past
passe-temps m hobby
passeport m passport
passer to pass ; to spend (time)
  se passer to happen
passerelle f gangway (bridge)
passionnant(e) exciting
passoire f sieve ; colander
pastèque f watermelon
pasteur m minister (of religion)
pastille f lozenge
pastis m aniseed-flavoured apéritif
pataugeoire f paddling pool
pâte f pastry ; dough ; paste
pâté m pâté
pâtes fpl pasta
patient(e) m/f patient (in hospital)
patin m skate
  patins à glace ice skates
  patins à roulettes roller skates
patinoire f skating rink
pâtisserie f cake shop ; little cake
patron m boss ; pattern (knitting, dress, etc)
patronne f boss
pauvre poor
payer to pay (for)
  payé(e) paid
  payé(e) d'avance prepaid
pays m land ; country
  du pays local
Pays-Bas mpl Netherlands
paysage m countryside ; scenery
péage m toll (motorway, etc)
peau f hide (leather) ; skin
pêche f peach ; fishing
pêcher to fish

pêcheur m angler
pédale f pedal
pédalo m pedal boat/pedalo
pédicure m/f chiropodist
peigne m comb
peignoir m dressing gown ; bathrobe
peindre to paint ; to decorate
peinture f painting ; paintwork
peler to peel (fruit)
pèlerinage m pilgrimage
pelle f spade
  pelle à poussière dustpan
pellicule f film (for camera)
  pellicule couleur colour film
  pellicule noir et blanc black and white film
pelote f ball (of string, wool)
  pelote basque pelota (ball game for 2 players)
pelouse f lawn
pencher to lean
pendant during
pendant que while
pénicilline f penicillin
péninsule f peninsula
pénis m penis
penser to think
pension f guesthouse
  pension complète full board
pente f slope
Pentecôte f Whitsun
pépin m pip
perceuse électrique f electric drill
perdre to lose
perdu(e) lost (object)
père m father
périmé(e) out of date
périphérique m ring road
perle f bead ; pearl
permanente f perm
permettre to permit (something)
permis m permit ; licence
  permis de chasse hunting permit
  permis de conduire driving licence
  permis de pêche fishing permit
perruque f wig
persil m parsley

p

personne f person
peser to weigh
pétanque f type of bowls
pétillant(e) fizzy
petit(e) small ; slight
  petit déjeuner breakfast
  petit pain roll
petit-fils m grandson
petite-fille f granddaughter
pétrole m oil (petroleum) ; paraffin
peu little ; few
  à peu près approximately
  un peu (de) a bit (of)
peur f fear
  avoir peur (de) to be afraid (of)
peut-être perhaps
phare m headlight ; lighthouse
pharmacie f chemist's ; pharmacy
phoque m seal (animal)
photo f photograph
photocopie f photocopy
photocopier to photocopy
piano m piano
pichet m jug ; carafe

p

pie f magpie
pièce f room (in house) ; play (theatre) ; coin
  pièce d'identité means of identification
  pièce de rechange spare part
pied m foot
  à pied on foot
pierre f stone

PIÉTONS pedestrians

pignon m pine kernel
pile f pile ; battery (for radio, etc)
pilon m drumstick (of chicken)
pilote m/f pilot
pilule f pill
pin m pine
pince f pliers
  pince à cheveux hairgrip
  pince à épiler tweezers
  pince à linge clothes peg
  pince à ongles nail clippers
pipe f pipe (smoking)
piquant(e) spicy ; hot
pique-nique m picnic

p

piquer to sting
piquet m peg (for tent)
piqûre f insect bite ; injection ; sting
pire worse
piscine f swimming pool
pissenlit m dandelion
pistache f pistachio (nut)
piste f ski-run ; runway (airport)
  piste cyclable cycle track
  piste de luge toboggan run
  piste pour débutants nursery slope
  pistes tous niveaux slopes for all levels of skiers
pistolet m pistol
placard m cupboard
place f square (in town) ; seat ; space (room)
  places debout standing room
plafond m ceiling
plage f beach
  plage seins nus topless beach
plainte f complaint
plaisanterie f joke
plaisir m enjoyment ; pleasure
plaît: s'il vous/te plaît please
plan m map (of town)
  plan de la ville street map
planche f plank
  planche à découper chopping board
  planche à repasser ironing board
  planche à voile sailboard ; windsurfing
  planche de surf surfboard
plancher m floor (of room)
plante f plant ; sole (of foot, shoe)
plaque f sheet ; plate
  plaque (d'immatriculation) f numberplate
plat m dish ; course (of meal)
  plat de résistance main course
  plat principal main course
  plats à emporter take-away meal
plat(e) level (surface) ; flat
  à plat flat (battery)
platane m plane tree

plateau m tray
platine laser f CD player
plâtre m plaster
plein(e) (de) full (of)
  plein! fill it up! (car)
  plein sud facing south
  plein tarif peak rate
pleurer to cry (weep)
pleuvoir to rain
  il pleut it's raining
plier to fold
plomb m lead ; fuse
plombage m filling (in tooth)
plombier m plumber
plonger to dive
pluie f rain
plume f feather
plus more ; most
  plus (de) more (than)
  plus grand(e) (que) bigger (than)
  plus tard later
plusieurs several
pneu m tyre
  pneu de rechange spare tyre
  pneu dégonflé flat tyre
  pneus cloutés snow tyres
poche f pocket
poché(e) poached
poêle f frying-pan
poème m poem
poids m weight
  poids lourd heavy goods vehicle
  poids maximum autorisé luggage allowance
poignée f handle
poignet m wrist
poil m hair ; coat (of animal)
poinçonner to punch (ticket, etc)
point m place ; point ; stitch ; dot
  à point medium rare (meat)
pointure f size (of shoes)
poire f pear ; pear brandy
poireau m leek
pois m pea ; spot (dot)
  petits pois peas
poison m poison
poisson m fish
poissonnerie f fishmonger's shop
poitrine f breast ; chest

poivre m pepper
poivron m pepper (capsicum)
police f policy (insurance) ; police
policier m policeman ; detective film/novel
pollué(e) polluted
pommade f ointment
pomme f apple ; potato
pomme de terre f potato
pompe f pump
pompes funèbres fpl undertaker's
pompier m fireman
  pompiers fire brigade
poney m pony
pont m bridge ; deck (of ship)
  faire le pont to have a long weekend
populaire popular
porc m pork ; pig
port m harbour ; port
portable m mobile phone ; laptop
portatif portable
porte f door ; gate
portefeuille m wallet
porter to wear; to carry
porte-bagages m luggage rack
porte-clefs m keyring
porte-monnaie m purse
porteur m porter
portier m doorman
portion f helping ; portion
porto m port (wine)
poser to put ; to lay down
posologie f dosage
posséder to own
poste f post ; post office
  poste de contrôle checkpoint
  poste de secours first-aid post
poste m radio/television set ; extension (phone)
poster m poster (decorative)
poster to post
pot m pot ; carton (yoghurt, etc)
  pot d'échappement exhaust pipe

POTABLE ok to drink

potage m soup
poteau m post (pole)
  poteau indicateur signpost

p

poterie f pottery
poubelle f dustbin
pouce m thumb
poudre f powder
poule f hen
poulet m chicken
poumon m lung
poupée f doll
pour for
pourboire m tip
pourquoi why
pourri(e) rotten (fruit, etc)
pousser to push
poussette f push chair

POUSSEZ push

poussière f dust
pouvoir to be able to
pré m meadow
préfecture de police f police
  headquarters
préféré(e) favourite
préférer to prefer
premier(-ière) first
  premier cru first-class wine
  premiers secours first aid
prendre to take ; to get ; to catch
prénom m first name
préparer to prepare ; to cook
près de near (to)
présenter to present ; to introduce
préservatif m condom
pressé(e) squeezed ; pressed
pressing m dry cleaner's
pression f pressure
  pression des pneus tyre pressure
prêt(e) ready
  prêt à cuire ready to cook
prêt-à-porter m ready-to-wear
prêter to lend
prêtre m priest
prévision f forecast
prier to pray

PRIÈRE DE... please...

prince m prince
princesse f princess
principal(e) main
printemps m spring

priorité f right of way
  priorité à droite give way to
  traffic from right
prise f plug ; socket

PRIVÉ private

prix m price ; prize
  à prix réduit cut-price
  prix d'entrée admission fee
  prix de détail retail price
probablement probably
problème m problem
prochain(e) next
proche close (near)
produits mpl produce ; product
professeur m teacher
profiter de to take advantage of
profond(e) deep
programme m schedule ; programme (list of performers, etc)
  programme informatique computer program
promenade f walk ; promenade ;
  ride (in vehicle)
  faire une promenade to go for
  a walk
promettre to promise
promotionnel(le) special low-price
prononcer to pronounce
propre clean ; own
propriétaire m/f owner
propriété f property
protège-slip m panty-liner
protestant(e) Protestant
provenance f origin ; source
provisions fpl groceries
province f province
provisoire temporary
provisoirement for the time being
proximité: à proximité nearby
prune f plum ; plum brandy
pruneau m prune ; damson (Switz.)
pruneau sec prune (Switz.)
public m audience
public(-que) public
publicité f advertisement (on TV)
puce f flea
puissance f power
puits m well (for water)

pull m sweater
pullover m sweater
purée f purée ; mashed
PV m parking ticket
pyjama m pyjamas

Q

qualifié(e) skilled
qualité f quality
quand when
quantité f quantity
  quantité tolérée customs
  allowance
quarantaine f quarantine
quart m quarter
quartier m neighbourhood ; district
que f than ; whom ; what
  qu'est-ce que c'est? what is it?
quel(le) which ; what
quelqu'un someone
quelque some
quelque chose something
quelquefois sometimes
question f question
queue f queue ; tail
  faire la queue to queue (up)
qui who ; which
quincaillerie f hardware ; hardware shop
quinzaine f fortnight
quitter to leave a place
quoi what
quotidien(ne) daily

R

rabais m reduction
raccourci m short cut
raccrocher to hang up (phone)
race f race (people)
racine f root
radeau de sauvetage m life raft
radiateur m radiator
radio f radio
radiographie f X-ray

radis m radish
rafraîchissements mpl refreshments
rage f rabies
ragoût m stew ; casserole
raide steep
raie f skate (fish)
raifort m horseradish
raisin m grape
  raisin sec sultana ; raisin ; currant
  raisins blancs green grapes
  raisins noirs black grapes
raison f reason

rallonge f extension (electrical)
randonnée f hike
  randonnée à cheval pony-
  trekking
râpe f grater
râpé(e) grated
rappeler to remind
  se rappeler to remember
rapide quick ; fast
rapide m express train
raquette f racket ; bat ; snowshoe
rare rare ; unusual
raser to shave off
  se raser to shave
rasoir m razor
rater to miss (train, flight etc)
RATP f Paris transport authority
rayé(e) striped
rayon m shelf ; department (in
  store) ; spoke (of wheel)
  rayon hommes menswear
RC ground floor
reboucher to recork
récemment recently
récepteur m receiver (of phone)
réception f reception ; check-in
réceptionniste m/f receptionist
recette f recipe
recharge f refill
rechargeable refillable (lighter, pen)
recharger to recharge (battery, etc)
réchaud de camping m camping
  stove
réclamation f complaint
réclame f advertisement

r

recommandé(e) registered (mail)
recommander to recommend
récompense f reward
reconnaître to recognize
reçu m receipt
réduction f reduction ; discount; concession
réduire to reduce
refuge m mountain hut
refuser to reject ; to refuse
regarder to look at
régime m diet (slimming)
région f region
règle f rule ; ruler (for measuring)
règles fpl period (menstruation)
  règles douloureuses cramps
règlement m regulation ; payment
régler to pay ; to settle
réglisse f liquorice
reine f queen
relais routier m roadside restaurant
rembourser to refund
remède m remedy
remercier to thank

r **remettre** to put back
  remettre à plus tard to postpone
  se remettre to recover (from illness)
remonte-pente m ski lift
remorque f trailer
remorquer to tow
remplir to fill ; to fill in/out/up
renard m fox
rencontrer to meet
rendez-vous m date ; appointment
rendre to give back
renouveler to renew

rentrée f return to work after break
  rentrée (des classes) start of the new school year
renverser to knock down (in car)
réparations fpl repairs
réparer to fix (repair)
repas m meal
repasser to iron
répondeur automatique m answerphone

répondre (à) to reply ; to answer
réponse f answer ; reply
repos m rest
  se reposer to rest
représentation f performance
requis(e) required
RER m Paris high-speed commuter train
réseau m network
réservation f reservation ; booking
réserve naturelle f nature reserve
réservé(e) reserved
réserver to book (reserve)
réservoir m tank
  réservoir d'essence fuel tank
respirer to breathe
ressort m spring (metal)
restaurant m restaurant
reste m rest (remainder)
rester to remain ; to stay
restoroute m roadside or motorway restaurant
retard m delay
retirer to withdraw ; to collect (tickets)
retour m return
retourner to go back
retrait m withdrawal ; collection
  retrait d'espèces cash withdrawal
retraité(e) retired
retraité(e) m/f old-age pensioner
rétrécir to shrink (clothes)
rétroviseur m rearview mirror
  rétroviseur latéral wing mirror
réunion f meeting
réussir (à) to succeed
réussite f success ; patience (game)
réveil m alarm clock
réveiller to wake (someone)
  se réveiller to wake up
réveillon m Christmas/New Year's Eve
revenir to come back
réverbère m lamppost
revue f review ; magazine

rhum m rum

rhumatisme m rheumatism
rhume m cold *(illness)*
  rhume des foins hay fever
riche rich
rideau m curtain
rides fpl wrinkles
rien nothing ; anything
  rien à déclarer nothing to declare
rire to laugh
rivage m shore
rive f river bank
rivière f river
riz m rice
RN see **route**
robe f gown ; dress
robinet m tap
rocade f ringroad
rocher m rock *(boulder)*
rognon m kidney *(to eat)*
roi m king
roman m novel
roman(e) Romanesque
romand(e) f French speaking (in Switzerland)
romantique romantic
romarin m rosemary
rond(e) round
rond-point m roundabout
rose pink
rose f rose
rossignol m nightingale
rôti(e) roast
rôtisserie f steakhouse ; roast meat counter
roue f wheel
  roue de secours spare wheel
rouge red
rouge à lèvres m lipstick
rouge-gorge m robin
rougeole f measles
rougeur f rash *(skin)*
rouillé(e) rusty
rouleau à pâtisserie m rolling pin
rouler to roll ; to go *(by car)*
route f road ; route
  route barrée road closed
  route nationale (RN) trunk-road
  route principale major road
  route secondaire minor road

routier m lorry driver
Royaume-Uni m United Kingdom
ruban m ribbon ; tape
rubéole f rubella, German measles
rue f street
  rue sans issue no through road
ruelle f lane ; alley
ruisseau m stream
russe Russian

S

SA Ltd ; plc
sable m sand
  sables mouvants quicksand
sabot de Denver wheel clamp
sac m sack ; bag
  sac à dos backpack
  sac à main handbag
  sac de couchage sleeping bag
  sac poubelle bin liner
sachet de thé m tea bag
sacoche f panniers *(for bike)*
safran m saffron
sage good *(well-behaved)* ; wise
saignant(e) rare *(steak)*
saigner to bleed
saint(e) m/f saint
Saint-Sylvestre f New Year's Eve
saisir to seize
saison f season
  basse saison low season
  de saison in season
  haute saison high season
saisonnier seasonal
salade f lettuce ; salad
  salade de fruits fruit salad
salaire m salary; wage
sale dirty
salé(e) salty ; savoury
salle f lounge *(at airport)* ; hall ; ward *(hospital)*
  salle à manger dining room
  salle d'attente waiting room
  salle de bains bathroom
salon m sitting room ; lounge
  salon de beauté beauty salon
salut! hi!

181

SAMEDI Saturday

sandales fpl sandals
sandwich m sandwich
sang m blood
sanglier m wild boar
sans without
  sans alcool alcohol-free
  sans connaissance unconscious
  sans issue no through road
santé f health
  santé! cheers!
  en bonne santé well (healthy)
sapin m fir (tree)
SARL f Ltd ; plc
sauce f sauce
sauf except (for)
saumon m salmon
sauter to jump
sauvegarder to back up (computer)
sauver to rescue
savoir to know (be aware of)
  savoir faire quelque chose to know how to do sth
savon m soap
Scellofrais® Clingfilm®
scène f stage
scie f saw
score m score (of match)
scotch m whisky
séance f meeting ; performance
seau bucket
sec (sèche) dried (fruit, beans)
sèche-cheveux m hairdryer
sèche-linge m tumble dryer
sécher to dry
seconde f second (in time)
  en seconde second class
secouer to shake
secours m help
secrétaire m/f secretary
secrétariat m office
secteur m sector ; mains
sécurité f security ; safety
séjour m stay ; visit
sel m salt
self m self-service restaurant
selle f saddle
semaine f week

sens m meaning ; direction
  sens interdit no entry
  sens unique one-way street
sentier m footpath
  sentier écologique nature trail
sentir to feel

SEPTEMBRE September

séparément separately
série f series ; set
seringue f syringe
serré(e) tight (fitting)
serrer to grip ; to squeeze
  serrez à droite keep to the right-hand lane
serrure f lock
serrurerie f locksmith's
serveur m waiter
serveuse f waitress
servez-vous help yourself
service m service ; service charge ; favour
  service compris service included
  service d'urgences accident & emergency dept
serviette f towel ; briefcase
  serviette hygiénique sanitary towel
servir to dish up ; to serve
seul(e) alone ; lonely
seulement only
sexe m sex
shampooing m shampoo
  shampooing et mise en plis shampoo and set
short m shorts
si if ; yes (to negative question)
SIDA m AIDS
siècle m century
siège m seat ; head office
  siège pour bébés/enfants car seat (for children)
signaler to report
signer to sign
simple simple ; single ; plain
site m site
  site web web site
situé(e) located
ski m ski ; skiing

ski de randonnée cross-country skiing

ski nautique water-skiing

slip m underpants ; panties

slip (de bain) trunks *(swimming)*

snack m snack bar

SNCB f Belgian railways

SNCF f French railways

société f company ; society

sœur f sister

soie f silk

soif f thirst

avoir soif to be thirsty

soin m care

soins du visage facial

soir m evening

soirée f evening ; party

soja m soya ; soya bean

sol m ground ; soil

soldat m soldier

solde m balance *(remainder owed)*

SOLDES sales

soldes permanents sale prices all year round

sole f sole *(fish)*

soleil m sun ; sunshine

somme f sum

sommelier m wine waiter

sommet m top *(of hill, mountain)*

somnifère m sleeping pill

sonner to ring ; to strike

sonnette f doorbell

SONNEZ ring

sorbet m water ice

sorte f kind *(sort, type)*

SORTIE exit

sortie de secours emergency exit

sortie interdite no exit

sortir to go out *(leave)*

soucoupe f saucer

soudain suddenly

souhaiter to wish

soûl(e) drunk

soulever to lift

soupape f valve

soupe f soup

souper m supper

sourcils mpl eyebrows

sourd(e) deaf

sourire to smile

souris f mouse *(also for computer)*

sous underneath ; under

SOUS-SOL basement

sous-titres mpl subtitles

sous-vêtements mpl underwear

souterrain(e) underground

soutien-gorge m bra

souvenir m memory ; souvenir

souvent often

sparadrap m sticking plaster

spécial(e) special

spécialité f speciality

spectacle m show *(in theatre)* ; entertainment

spectateurs mpl audience

spiritueux mpl spirits

sport m sport

sports nautiques water sports

sportif(-ive) sports ; athletic

stade m stadium

stage m course *(period of training)*

standard m switchboard

station f station *(metro)* ; resort

station balnéaire seaside resort

station de taxis taxi rank

station thermale spa

station-service service station

stationnement m parking

stérilet m coil *(IUD)*

stimulateur (cardiaque) m pacemaker

store m blind ; awning

stylo m pen

sucette f lollipop ; dummy

sucre m sugar

sucré(e) sweet

sud m south

suisse Swiss

Suisse f Switzerland

suite f series ; continuation ; sequel

suivant(e) following

suivre to follow

faire suivre please forward

super m four-star petrol

s

supermarché m supermarket
supplément m extra charge
supplémentaire extra
sur on ; onto ; on top of ; upon
  sur place on the spot
sûr safe ; sure
surcharger to overload
surchauffer to overheat
surf m surfing
  faire du surf to surf
  surf des neiges snowboard
  surf sur neige snowboarding
surgelés mpl frozen foods
surveillé(e) supervised
survêtement m tracksuit
sympa(thique) nice ; pleasant
synagogue f sysnagogue
syndicat d'initiative m tourist
  office

T

t

tabac m tobacco ; tobacconist's
table f table
tableau m painting ; picture ; board
  tableau de bord dashboard
tablier m apron
tache f stain
taie d'oreiller f pillowcase
taille f size (of clothes) ; waist
  taille unique one size
  grande taille outsize (clothes)
tailleur m tailor ; suit (women's)
talc m talc
talon m heel ; stub (counterfoil)
  talon minute shoes reheeled
  while you wait
tampon m tampon
  tampon Jex® scouring pad
tante f aunt
taper to strike ; to type
tapis m carpet
  tapis de sol groundsheet
tard late
  au plus tard at the latest
tarif m price-list ; rate ; tarif
tarte f flan ; tart
tartine f slice of bread and butter
  (or jam)

tartiner: à tartiner for spreading
tasse f cup ; mug
taureau m bull
tauromachie f bull-fighting
taux m rate
  taux de change exchange rate
  taux fixe flat rate
taxe f duty ; tax (on goods)
taxi m cab (taxi)
TCF m Touring Club de France (AA)
teinture f dye
teinturerie f dry cleaner's
télé f TV
télébenne f gondola lift
télécabine f gondola lift
télécarte f phonecard
télécommande f remote control
téléphérique m cable-car
téléphone m telephone
  téléphone portable mobile
  phone
téléphoner (à) to phone
téléphoniste m/f operator
télésiège m chair-lift
téléviseur m television (set)
télévision f television
température f temperature
tempête f storm
temple m temple ; synagogue ;
  protestant church
temps m weather ; time
tendon m tendon
tenir to hold ; to keep
tennis m tennis
tension f voltage ; blood pressure
tente f tent
tenue f clothes ; dress
  tenue de soirée evening dress
terrain m ground ; land ; pitch ;
  course (golf)
terrasse f terrace
terre f land ; earth ; ground
  terre cuite terracotta
tête f head
tétine f dummy (for baby)
TGV m high-speed train
thé m tea
  thé au lait tea with milk
  thé nature tea without milk

théâtre m theatre
théière f teapot
thermomètre m thermometer
ticket m ticket *(bus, cinema, museum)*
  ticket de caisse receipt
tiède lukewarm
tiers m third ; third party
timbre m stamp
tirage m printing ; print *(photo)*
  tirage le mercredi lottery draw
  on Wednesdays
tire-bouchon m corkscrew
tirer to pull

tiroir m drawer
tisane f herbal tea
tissu m material ; fabric
titre m title
  à titre indicatif for info only
  à titre provisoire provisionally
titulaire m/f holder of *(card, etc)*
toile f canvas ; web *(spider)*
toilettes fpl toilet ; powder room
toit m roof
  toit ouvrant sunroof
tomate f tomato
tomber to fall
tonalité f dialling tone
tongs fpl flip flops
tonneau m barrel *(wine/beer)*
tonnerre m thunder
torchon m tea towel
tordre to twist
tôt early
total m total *(amount)*
toucher to touch
toujours always ; still ; forever
tour f tower
tour m trip ; walk ; ride
tourisme m sightseeing
touriste m/f tourist
touristique tourist *(route, resort, etc)*
tourner to turn
tournesol m sunflower
tournevis m screwdriver
  tournevis cruciforme phillips
  screwdriver
tourte f pie

tous all *(plural)*
  tous les jours daily *(each day)*
Toussaint f All Saints' Day
tousser to cough
tout(e) all ; everything
  tout à l'heure in a while
  tout compris all inclusive
  tout de suite straight away
  tout droit straight ahead
  toute la journée all day
tout le monde everyone
toutes all *(plural)*
  toutes directions all routes
toux f cough
tradition f custom *(tradition)*
traditionnel(-elle) traditional
traduction f translation
traduire to translate
train m train
trajet m journey
tramway m tram
tranchant sharp *(razor, knife)*
tranche f slice
tranquille quiet *(place)*
transférer to transfer
transpirer to sweat
travail m work
travailler to work *(person)*
  travailler à son compte to be
  self employed
travaux mpl road works
travers: à travers through
traversée f crossing *(voyage)*
traverser to cross *(road, sea, etc)*
tremplin m diving-board
  tremplin de ski ski jump
très very ; much
triangle de présignalisation m
  warning triangle
tricot m knitting ; sweater
tricoter to knit
trimestre m term
triste sad
trop too ; too much
trottoir m pavement ; sidewalk
trou m hole
trousse f pencil case
  trousse de premiers secours
  first aid kit

t

trouver to find
  se trouver to be *(situated)*
tuer kill
tunnel m tunnel
tuyau m pipe *(for water, gas)*
  tuyau d'arrosage hosepipe
TVA f VAT
typique typical

U

UE f EU (European Union)
ulcère m ulcer
ultérieur(e) later *(date, etc)*
un(e) one ; a ; an
  l'un ou l'autre either one
uni(e) plain *(not patterned)*
Union européenne f European
  Union
université f university
urgence f urgency ; emergency
urine f urine
usage m use
usine f factory
utile useful
utiliser to use

u

V

vacances fpl holiday(s)
  en vacances on holiday
  grandes vacances summer holiday
vaccin m vaccination
vache f cow
vagin m vagina
vague f wave *(on sea)*
vaisselle f crockery
valable valid *(ticket, licence, etc)*
valeur f value
valider to validate
valise f suitcase
vallée f valley
valoir to be worth
  ça vaut... it's worth...
vanille f vanilla
vapeur f steam
varicelle f chickenpox

v

varié(e) varied ; various
vase m vase
veau m calf ; veal
vedette f speedboat ; star *(film)*
végétal(e) vegetable
végétarien(ne) vegetarian
véhicule m vehicle
  véhicules lents slow-moving
  vehicles
veille f the day before ; eve
  veille de Noël Christmas Eve
veine f vein
vélo m bike
  vélo tout terrain (VTT) mountain bike
velours m velvet
venaison f venison
vendange(s) fpl harvest *(of grapes)*
vendeur(-euse) m/f sales assistant
vendre to sell

  À VENDRE for sale

  VENDREDI Friday

  vendredi saint Good Friday
vénéneux poisonous
venir to come
vent m wind
vente f sale
  vente aux enchères auction
  vente-sauvage car boot sale
ventilateur m ventilator ; fan
verglas m black ice
vérifier to check ; to audit
vernis m varnish
  vernis à ongles nail varnish
verre m glass
  verres de contact contact lenses
verrouillage central m central
  locking
vers toward(s) ; about
versement m payment ; instalment
verser to pour ; to pay
vert(e) green
veste f jacket
vestiaire m cloakroom
vêtements mpl clothes
vétérinaire m/f vet
veuf m widower

veuillez... please...
veuve f widow
via by (via)
viande f meat
  viande hachée mince (meat)
vidange f oil change (car)
vide empty
videoclub m video shop
vie f life
vieux (vieille) old
vigile m security guard
vigne f vine ; vineyard
vignoble m vineyard
VIH m HIV
village m village
ville f town ; city
vin m wine
  vin du cru locally grown wine
  vin pétillant sparkling wine
vinaigre m vinegar
violer to rape
violet(-ette) purple
vipère f adder ; viper
virage m bend ; curve ; corner
vis f screw
  vis platinées points (in car)
visage m face
visite f visit ; consultation (of doctor)
  visite guidée guided tour
visiter to visit (a place)
visiteur(-euse) m/f visitor
visser to screw on
vite quickly ; fast
vitesse f gear (of car) ; speed
  vitesse limitée à... speed limit...
vitrail m stained-glass window
vitrine f shop window
vivre to live
VO: en VO with subtitles (film)
vœu m wish
voici here is/are
voie f lane (of road) ; line ; track
voilà there is/are
voile f sail ; sailing
voilier m sailing boat
voir to see
voisin(e) m/f neighbour
voiture f car ; coach (of train)
vol m flight ; theft

vol intérieur domestic flight
volaille f poultry
volant m steering wheel
voler to fly (bird) ; to steal
volet m shutter (on window)
voleur(-euse) m/f thief
volonté f will
  à volonté as much as you like
vomir to vomit
v.o.s.t. original version with
  subtitles (film)
vouloir to want
voyage m journey
  voyage d'affaires business trip
  voyage organisé package holiday
voyager to travel
voyageur(-euse) m/f traveller
vrai(e) real ; true
VTT m mountain bike
vue f view ; sight

V

W

w-c mpl toilet
wagon m carriage ; waggon
wagon-couchettes m sleeping car
wagon-restaurant m dining car
web m internet

X

xérès m sherry

Y

yacht m yacht
yaourt m yoghurt
  yaourt nature plain yoghurt
yeux mpl eyes
youyou m dinghy

Z

zéro m zero
zona m shingles (illness)
zone f zone
  zone piétonne pedestrian area
zoo m zoo

NOUNS

Unlike English, French nouns have a gender: they are either masculine (**le**) or feminine (**la**). Therefore words for *the* and *a(n)* must agree with the noun they accompany – whether *masculine, feminine* or *plural*:

	masc.	*fem.*	*plural*
the	**le chat**	**la rue**	**les chats, les rues**
a, an	**un chat**	**une rue**	**des chats, des rues**

If the noun begins with a vowel (**a, e, i, o** or **u**) or an unsounded **h**, **le** and **la** shorten to **l'**, i.e. **l'avion** *(m)*, **l'école** *(f)*, **l'hôtel** *(m)*.

NOTE: le and **les** used after the prepositions **à** (to, at) and **de** (any, some, of) contract as follows:

à + **le** = **au** (**au cinéma** but **à la gare**)
à + **les** = **aux** (**aux magasins** - applies to both *(m)* and *(f)*)
de + **le** = **du** (**du pain** but **de la confiture**)
de + **les** = **des** (**des pommes** - applies to both *(m)* and *(f)*)

There are some broad rules as to noun endings which indicate whether they are *masculine* or *feminine*:

Generally *masculine* endings: -**er**, -**ier**, -**eau**, -**t**, -**c**, -**age**, -**ail**, -**oir**, -**é**, -**on**, -**acle**, -**ège**, -**ème**, -**o**, -**ou**.

Generally *feminine* endings: -**euse**, -**trice**, -**ère**, -**ière**, -**elle**, -**te**, -**tte**, -**de**, -**che**, -**age**, -**aille**, -**oire**, -**ée**, -**té**, -**tié**, -**onne**, -**aison**, -**ion**, -**esse**, -**ie**, -**ine**, -**une**, -**ure**, -**ance**, -**anse**, -**ence**, -**ense**.

THE FORMATION OF PLURALS

The general rule is to add an **s** to the singular:

le chat → **les chats**

Exceptions occur with the following noun endings: -**eau**, -**eu**, -**al**

le bat<u>eau</u> → **les bat<u>eaux</u>**
le nev<u>eu</u> → **les nev<u>eux</u>**
le chev<u>al</u> → **les chev<u>aux</u>**

Nouns ending in **s**, **x**, or **z** do not change in the plural.

le dos → **les dos**
le prix → **les prix**
le nez → **les nez**

ADJECTIVES

Adjectives normally follow the noun they describe in French,

e.g.   **la pomme verte** (the green apple)

Some common exceptions which precede the noun are: **beau** beautiful, **bon** good, **grand** big, **haut** high, **jeune** young, **long** long, **joli** pretty, **mauvais** bad, **nouveau** new, **petit** small, **vieux** old.

e.g.   **un bon livre** (a good book)

French adjectives have to reflect the gender of the noun they describe. To make an adjective feminine, an **e** is added to the *masculine* form (where this does not already end in an **e**, e.g. **jeune**). A final consonant, which is usually silent in the *masculine* form, is pronounced in the *feminine*:

masc. **le livre vert**   *fem.* **la pomme verte**
  luh leevr vehr   *la pom vehrt*
  (the green book)   (the green apple)

To make an adjective plural, an **s** is added to the singular form: *masculine plural* – **verts** (remember – the ending is still silent: *vehr*) or *feminine plural* – **vertes** (because of the **e**, the **t** ending is sounded: *vehrt*).

MY, YOUR, HIS, HER

These words also depend on the gender and number of the noun they accompany and not on the sex of the 'owner'.

	with masc. sing. noun	with fem. sing. noun	with plural nouns
my	**mon**	**ma**	**mes**
your *(familiar, singular)*	**ton**	**ta**	**tes**
his/her	**son**	**sa**	**ses**
our	**notre**	**notre**	**nos**
your *(polite and plural)*	**votre**	**votre**	**vos**
their	**leur**	**leur**	**leurs**

PRONOUNS

subject		*object*	
I	**je, j'**	me	**me, m'**
you *(familiar)*	**tu**	you	**te, t'**
you *(polite and plural)*	**vous**	you	**vous**
he/it	**il**	him/it	**le, l'**
she/it	**elle**	her/it	**la, l'**
we	**nous**	us	**nous**
they *(masc.)*	**ils**	them	**les**
they *(fem.)*	**elles**	them	**les**

g
r
a
m
m
a
r

In French there are two forms of *you* – **tu** and **vous**. Tu is the familiar form which is used with children and people you know as friends. **Vous**, as well as being the plural form for *you*, is also the polite form of addressing someone. You should probably use this form until the other person invites you to use the more familiar **tu** ("on se dit 'tu'?").

Object pronouns are placed before the verb:

e.g.   **il vous aime** (he loves <u>you</u>)
         nous la connaissons (we know <u>her</u>)

However, in commands or requests, object pronouns follow the verb,

e.g.   **écoutez-le** (listen to <u>him</u>)
         aidez-moi (help <u>me</u>)

NOTE: this does not apply to negative commands or requests,

e.g.   **ne le faites pas** (don't do <u>it</u>)

The object pronouns shown above are also used to mean **to me**, **to us**, etc. except,

e.g.   **le** and **la** become **lui** (to him, to her)
         les becomes **leur** (to them)
         il le lui donne (he gives it <u>to him</u>)

VERBS

There are three main patterns of endings for verbs in French – those ending **-er**, **-ir** and **-re** in the dictionary.

DONN<u>ER</u>	TO GIVE
je donne	I give
tu donnes	you give
il/elle donne	he/she gives
nous donnons	we give
vous donnez	you give
ils/elles donnent	they give

FIN<u>IR</u>	TO FINISH
je finis	I finish
tu finis	you finish
il/elle finit	he/she finishes
nous finissons	we finish
vous finissez	you finish
ils/elles finissent	they finish

RÉPONDRE / TO REPLY

RÉPONDRE	TO REPLY
je réponds	I reply
tu réponds	you reply
il/elle répond	he/she replies
nous répondons	we reply
vous répondez	you reply
ils/elles répondent	they reply

IRREGULAR VERBS

Among the most important irregular verbs are the following:

ÊTRE	TO BE	AVOIR	TO HAVE
je suis	I am	j'ai	I have
tu es	you are	tu as	you have
il/elle est	he/she is	il/elle a	he/she has
nous sommes	we are	nous avons	we have
vous êtes	you are	vous avez	you have
ils/elles sont	they are	ils/elles ont	they have

ALLER	TO GO	VENIR	TO COME
je vais	I go	je viens	I come
tu vas	you go	tu viens	you come
il/elle va	he/she goes	il/elle vient	he/she comes
nous allons	we go	nous venons	we come
vous allez	you go	vous venez	you come
ils/elles vont	they go	ils/elles viennent	they come

FAIRE	TO DO	VOULOIR	TO WANT
je fais	I do	je veux	I want
tu fais	you do	tu veux	you want
il/elle fait	he/she does	il/elle veut	he/she wants
nous faisons	we do	nous voulons	we want
vous faites	you do	vous voulez	you want
ils/elles font	they do	ils/elles veulent	they want

POUVOIR	TO BE ABLE TO	DEVOIR	TO HAVE TO
je peux	I can	je dois	I have to
tu peux	you can	tu dois	you have to
il/elle peut	he/she can	il/elle doit	he/she has to
nous pouvons	we can	nous devons	we have to
vous pouvez	you can	vous devez	you have to
ils/elles peuvent	they can	ils/elles doivent	they have to

PAST TENSE

To form the simple past tense, *I gave/I have given, I finished/I have finished*, combine the present tense of the verb **avoir** – *to have* with the past participle of the verb (**donné, fini, répondu**),

e.g.
j'ai donné	I gave/I have given
j'ai fini	I finished/I have finished
j'ai répondu	I replied/I have replied

Not all verbs take **avoir** (**j'ai...**, **il a...**) as their auxiliary verb. The reflexive verbs (**s'amuser**, **se promener**, etc) take **être** (**je suis...**, **il est...**), and so do a dozen or so other verbs which generally express the idea of motion or staying such as **aller** (to go) and **rester** (to stay),

e.g.
je me suis amusé	I had fun
je suis allé	I went
je suis resté	I stayed

When the auxiliary verb **être** is used, the past participle (**amusé**, **allé**, **resté**, etc) becomes adjectival and agrees with the subject of the verb in number and gender:

e.g.
je me suis amusée	I had fun *(female)*
nous nous sommes amusés	we had fun *(plural)*
je suis allée	I went *(female)*
nous sommes allés	we went *(plural)*
je suis restée	I stayed *(female)*
nous sommes restés	we stayed *(plural)*